HAPPY Na[...]
THE YEAR [...] [...]ON.

YOUR TEACHING [...] [...]

EVERY SUCCESS IN YOUR
POST UNIVERSITY LIFE AND
CAREER ENDEAVOURS.

EVENT INDUSTRY
BOSS

Eve Liett   Ioannis Soileuetsotis

Marge Bow   Milan Todorovic

Ela Rypers

Stephen Holt

PRAISE FOR JASON MACE AND GALA TENT LTD

"We wouldn't have had the success we had if it wasn't for Gala... We're not just a race winning team, we're also a good looking team."
- Zak Brown, United Autosports

"When Jason Mace talks about the Event Industry, you sit up and take note... A valuable guide for any aspiring entrepreneur."
- Sir Dave Richards, Former Chairman of the FA Premier League

"Jason has been supporting my events for years, and always provides a first class service."
- Peter Jones, Dragon's Den

"I wouldn't be back in racing if it wasn't for Gala Tent."
- Christian England, 2016 European Le Mans Series Champion

Jason is one of the most engaging and infectious entrepreneurs I know."
- Dame Julie Kenny

EVENT INDUSTRY BOSS

The Secret to Becoming Successful
In the Event Industry

JASON MACE

EVENT INDUSTRY BOSS

THE SECRET TO BECOMING SUCCESSFUL IN THE EVENT INDUSTRY

©Jason Mace 2019

CONTENTS

Section Two: Case Studies

Section Three: The Legal Stuff

JASON MACE
Honours and Awards

Yorkshire 42 Under 42 Award - **2011**

Chamber of Commerce

Entrepreneur of the Year – **2011**

Business Growth Award – **2011**

Manufacturing Excellence Award – **2012**

Innovation & Technology Award – **2012**

Business Person of the Year – **2012, 2013, 2014**

Digital and Creative Award - **2015**

Acquisition International

Deal of the Year Award – **2014**

UK IT Awards

Security Innovation of the Year Award – **2014**

Business Excellence Awards

Event Management Company of the Year - **2014**

Export Business of the Year - **2014**

2

ACQ5 Global Awards

Small Business of the Year – **2014**

Digital Entrepreneur Awards

Digital Team of the Year – **2015**

Insider International Trade Awards

International Company of the Year (up to £10m Turnover) – **2015**

UK Contact Centre Forum Awards

Best Use of Technology in a Contact Centre – **2018**

Call & Contact Centre Expo Awards

Security Solution of the Year - **2019**

PCI: Award for Excellence – **2019**

CNP Awards

Best International CNP Program - **2019**

INTRODUCTION

JASON MACE is a multi-award winning entrepreneur, whose speciality is supplying a range of products and services to the event industry. He has first hand knowledge in business management and marketing, with a portfolio of successful companies generating over £10m in sales each year. His net worth, built up from shrewd investments in companies, residential and commercial properties, bars and restaurants, stocks, machinery, trademarks, patents and financial technology, is estimated at over £20m.

His company Gala Tent is responsible for completely changing the landscape of the event industry by developing commercial marquees and accessories that are suitable for the garden marquee hire industry, which has grown into a very lucrative market for business start-ups. With a quick return on investment, the profit margin is unrivalled by any other industry, and now Jason is proactively looking for more enthusiastic entrepreneurs to work with worldwide. Maybe that person is you? With vision, hard work, and a little help, you can become the next successful supplier in the exciting world of the event industry.

Despite all the doom and gloom of the recent recession and the uncertainty caused by Brexit, this hasn't stopped people setting up their own companies. Figures suggest that around 600,000 new businesses emerge in the UK every year, and in 2016, Companies House reported that **almost 660,000** new start-ups were launched across the UK, which was up from 608,000 in 2015, and in 2018 it was estimated that small businesses accounted for at least 99.5% of all companies in every main industry sector. If you've got a dream business plan and you want to make it as an entrepreneur, the event industry is an exciting place to start, with a quick return on investment.

Armed with your ambition, a fantastic business partner in Gala Tent, and this useful guide to building success within the events industry, has there ever been a better time to become your own boss?

SECTION ONE:

The Guide to Becoming Successful in the Event Industry

THE MASTER SALESPERSON

A skilled sales role is the most rewarding job of all. Why you ask? If you have the skill to sell and make a deal you will never be out of work, you will always be able to feed yourself and your family. People who work in sales are always the highest paid members of staff, effectively writing their own pay-cheque, as commission on sales is usually uncapped! In sales, the work you put in is instantly rewarded on your monthly income. You may be selling the same or similar product or service each time, but no sale is the same, you meet many different and interesting people from all walks of life and encounter lifelong connections and even close friends. Plus, you will have lots of fun along the way.

Stop for a moment and take a good look around you... The chair you sit on, the table you eat at, the sofa you relax on and the car you drive were sold to you by a sales person. Without talented sales people we wouldn't have an economy, the world would soon come to a standstill and the markets would crash. This is how important the sales person is in today's economy.

Everyone is born a master salesman and you start from a very early age before you can even talk. For example, if your mother takes your dummy out you start crying to have it back, it's not long before you get your own way, is it? Later you are walking through the park with your parents. You see an ice cream van and want an ice cream. You ask Mum, "Can I have an ice cream?" She replies, "No, you will spoil your lunch."

Do you take no for answer? I think not, and a bout of kicking, screaming and sitting down in protest is in order!

Later, you ask for permission to stay out at your friend's house, Mum says, "No, it's a school night," so you go to dad for approval with a different story and approach, to convince your dad to override mum's decision to say its ok; this is what is called finding the decision maker and making a conversion. The next day you ask Dad for some pocket money to go to the cinema, Dad says, "No, you've had your pocket money. "

You then go to mum and add to the story. Eventually you will get what you want, as even at an early age you know it's a numbers game.

Children are such good sales people that sometimes they don't even need a reason to explain their wants and needs they just say, "Because!"

Brilliant!

Because *because* is actually the most powerful word in the English dictionary. So why is it that we lose this natural power of persuasion as we get older? This is easy to explain, we develop social fear and doubt, fear of rejection and fear of embarrassment. We doubt our ability of what really comes natural to us and our natural skill that we have unconsciously developed and mastered throughout our early life experiences is lost.

There is only 20% of the population that does not lose this ability, and those that make up this 20% are the high achievers, the ones that find life easy and have everything in abundance.

So now you know you have this skill you just need to re-harness your natural ability with awareness, persistence and ambition, you will soon realise that your ability is limitless. This will also have a positive effect on all other aspects of your life. For example, you may want to buy a certain type of car, a bigger house or a certain someone special in your life? What is stopping you? Work towards your goals set the bar high and start selling!

Famous quotes to think about:
- "Fortune favours the brave."
- "Knowing is not enough; we must apply. Willing is not enough; we must do."
- "Nothing great was ever achieved without enthusiasm."

WHY BE YOUR OWN EVENT INDUSTRY BOSS?

Many entrepreneurs consider themselves to be a person that likes to take control and make important decisions. In other words, owning a business saves them from having to work for anyone else. It gives the ability to direct the culture of your company. When you're in the driver's seat, you are making the decisions on how to steer your company into the future. This might be overwhelming for some, and one must know when and how best to delegate, but when you are able to make your own decisions about how you want to operate on a day-to-day basis, this enables you to create your own culture, your own brand and your own organisation, which in turn creates a solid future for you and a legacy for your family.

One of the main benefits of owning your own business is the flexibility that comes with it; setting your own hours, working from home, even taking your pets to work with you. Another benefit that can be just as important is that it lets you set your priorities and accomplish your wants and needs.

When you are your own boss, you are able to create your own schedule, which allows you to enjoy life and fulfil lifetime goals with your loved ones, who may be the inspiration and driving force behind your company. Running your own company as opposed to working for someone else is the sense of pride you establish in building something of your own. There is nothing like succeeding as a result of your own leadership, ideas, abilities and efforts. You may even get to travel the world in the name of your business if your company becomes an international enterprise.

Of course, you may be working many more hours in the long run, as when it comes to running your own business, it becomes your baby. You can never switch off and you're always on call. But then again, does this make it anymore different to many other jobs if you're ambitious and career driven? If you have this book in your hands then I'll assume you are. At least when you're your own boss, the beneficiary of your efforts, is you and you alone.

When you work for someone else, you rarely get to choose whom you work with. You can often spend more time with your colleagues than you do your own family, and if you have to spend over eight hours a day with co-workers that you don't get along with then how can you enjoy your job? That's not the case when you own your own business, since you get to make the decisions about who to hire (and fire). Over the years, I've hired dozens of personal friends, family members and former business colleagues to work with me in different capacities. Surround yourself with positive people who give you the confidence and optimism you need to keep moving forward. Weed out the people that put out negative vibes. The smaller your organisation is, the larger the choice that you have about who you work with. Some people thrive on the routine of their job, and enjoy the security a permanent job brings. These are the people you need to find to work with you.

There's no question that owning your own business is a risky proposition. But, with risk comes reward, the better you are at managing risk, the more rewards you can reap. The thing I enjoy most about the company is playing the 'game' of business. I like having my own money at risk, then having to live with the consequences of my decisions (good or bad). Like every other great game, the more you play, the better you become. Making things happen gives me a massive buzz to know that I did it, and that I was the first. There are an unlimited number of possibilities in almost every aspect of business, and as soon as you think you have things under control, everything changes and develops further. It is especially true in today's world of business, with the rapid rate of digital and technological evolution, so keep up!

As an entrepreneur, you can bet that each day will be filled with new opportunities to challenge yourself, to be creative and to learn something new. The great thing about owning a small business is I rarely experience the same day twice because every day, I learn something new about the act of owning a business. Whether it's something about taxes, accounting, sales methods or the latest technology, I am always fascinated by the pieces of knowledge that I learn every day just to keep the business on track. If you embrace these things and strive to understand every aspect of what makes your business tick, then you're already well on your way to success.

Many entrepreneurs say the long hours they invest in growing their business don't feel like long hours, and it's true, but don't let it burn you out. The fight of a new business start-up can be cruel, so learn to delegate and fast, get a partner on board if you can, pass some work out and ask for help. Don't let yourself hit a wall.

Be proactive; small companies can move fast. Don't leave work sitting in your basket at the end of the day, make sure it's empty and you have planned the following day before you go home. Follow up sales calls, customer service, accounts, or marketing. Never underestimate your ability to be proactive.

There are few things that entrepreneurs enjoy more than when they get to interact with their customers. Rather than hiding behind a series of automated greetings, small business owners thrive on dealing one-to-one with their best clients, usually in a meeting or even over a steak dinner. As a business owner, you can even make the decision to get rid of bad customers. You don't have to deal with customers who are unreasonable or just a pain in the backside, and we will cover this later in the book.

Embrace the idea of philanthropy. Many entrepreneurs love the idea of working in their community, including myself. Undertaking voluntary work can prove one of the most rewarding experiences of your career. You'll meet a wealth of interesting people who will inspire you and add value to your life. Make sure that this activity goes hand in hand with your company profile and it will show good character to your peers and prospective clients alike. Businessmen, celebrities and even politicians often enjoy volunteering stints, so why shouldn't you? Encourage your employees to also lend a hand and give back to your community by seeking out local projects. On top of the PR value that comes with such activity, the good feeling it can generate is priceless.

YOU + YOUR COMMUNITY
=VALUABLE PR

PERSONAL DEVELOPMENT

Before we go into the logistics of starting your own Event Industry business, let's look at how you can develop personally to give your company the greatest possible chance of success. This chapter contains information and advice that is designed to help you to think about your Personal Development and ways in which you can work towards goals and reaching your full potential.

Although early life development and early school, employment and family experiences can help to shape us as adults, Personal Development should be an ongoing part of your life.

Hopefully this chapter will help you to identify the skills you need to set life goals which can enhance your business prospects, raise your confidence, and lead to a more fulfilling, higher quality of life. Plan to make relevant, positive and effective life choices and decisions for your future.

So, Personal Development. I do this every day for at least twenty minutes and I advise all my staff to do the same. I even write this in every employment service level agreement that's committed to by my employees. I ask them to commit to thirty five hours a year of Personal

Development at a minimum. The reason I write this in my employment contracts is because I learnt this from my own Personal Development experience. For example, my wife is a veterinary surgeon and in her service level agreement she must study to keep her licence to practice. She must study to keep up with new procedures and protocols, and she signs up for a vet magazine every month, takes online courses and all of this is unpaid work. However, is she on a minimum wage? Not a chance. Doctors are high earners and you can be a doctor in any subject you choose but you aren't born a doctor. You must study to get there.

So, my theory is that this should be so in every industry, not just Doctors, right? Everyone should be responsible for improving their own skills. Unless you are a child, education doesn't come to you. YOU must be responsible for putting yourself in further education.

And guess what? The employees at Gala Tent that do progress the fastest, are the ones that perform some sort of Personal Development, as they can add more value to the business. And anyone can do this, whether you are employed or self-employed. If you are employed by somebody else then you can add £2,000 to your salary every year with Personal Development. If you are a business owner you can add a million pounds to the turnover. I know from experience that this is true, having achieved it during 2010 to 2011, during a recession, after studying marketing and Public Relations. I increased the turnover of Gala Tent by £1.1m and for my efforts, I won an Entrepreneur of the Year Award, which I'm very proud of.

Personal Development should be a lifelong process. Every day is a school day if you're smart enough to chase education. If you stop learning, you stop earning, it's that simple.

In the fast-moving world of Internet and technology, things change quickly, and you must keep up. You need skills, and lots of them. At Gala Tent, I have worked in every department and set up scripts, procedures, systems and protocol then trained someone else to take over the role. And when I say every department, I mean every. As I developed my company, I experienced a life working tirelessly in sales, customer service, PR and marketing, warehouse, procurement, accounts and the legal stuff. This means studying and lots of Personal Development.

So how did I do this? For example, when I set up the marketing department, I purchased lots of books on marketing and PR and even employed a marketing company for a short time to learn from them and then I did it myself. I then set up a marketing department and developed systems required to run a successful operation. Unless you study, you will never achieve this or maximise your potential.

The extent to which people can develop depends on certain needs being met at a particular time on their business or personal journey. Only when one level of need is satisfied, can a higher one be developed. We all crave the needs for safety and security in both the physical and economic sense. Progression is very satisfying and with it brings rewards and awards. Personal Development can be fun. Most of us, however, find it easier to motivate ourselves to learn and improve if we know why we are doing so, and have a clear idea of where we want to be in a few months or years.

Once you know where you want to be, the time comes to plan exactly how you'll get there. Drawing up a Personal Development plan is not essential, but it can help. Or alternatively, just do what I did and buy a few books on what you want to learn more about. It really is that simple. If you go to college they will only hand you out a list of books to study to pass an exam, right? You really don't need a teacher to tell you that. Let me be your teacher today; simply go online and order some tutorials, some examples of which are at the end of this chapter.

It is a good idea to keep a record of your Personal Development and make notes, I write and save Word documents a lot, and implement the theories and practices I discover or create in staff training later down the line. So, write down key points of interest in your learning as and when they occur, and you will be able to reflect on these at a later date. This reflection may well help to motivate you to learn more skills in the future. Try keeping a learning log or journal as you develop your skills and knowledge.

For more effective learning, it is important to reflect on your experience, and consider what you have learnt from it. Have a regular review of your Personal Development plans, and your development activities. This will ensure that you learn from what you have done. It will also ensure that your activities continue to move you towards your goals, and that your goals or vision remain relevant to you and your business.

Technology is great and nowadays you don't even have to read; you can download an audio book. My journey to work in the morning is around forty five minutes, which is a great amount of time to hook up my smart phone to the Bluetooth stereo in my 4x4 and listen to whatever I'm studying at that point. I like to go for a long walk, or when I go out for a five mile run I will stick in the headphones and study. Then in the evening before I go to sleep, I will read a chapter in a hard copy book, which would usually involve sales and marketing, or a biography of a public figure whose journey inspires me. I have a huge library of books I have accumulated over the years, all in my mission to better myself mentally and professionally. I've devoured the biographies of all of the Dragon's Den entrepreneurs, because if I know what they all know that makes me a super Dragon, right?

YouTube is also a good forum for knowledge and learning, you can type something like *Improve my sales* in to YouTube, and suddenly before your eyes are all sorts of videos with some very hot tips. This is free education. There is no excuse for not being educated these days. Everything you need to know is online or in a book, just ask Google. You can source as much or as little information as you want from online search engines from your sofa. You don't even need to use your fingers anymore. You can call out to your home hub device from the kitchen and be presented with all the free education you could ever need. It's that easy.

LinkedIn also has a new learning area, check this out its very good, successful professionals from all over the world share their knowledge and expertise and there are some great case studies to learn from.

So, a few I would recommend after you've finished this book would be:

- Anthony Robbins
- Jim Rohn
- Zig Ziglar

All of the above will all provide you with some value that you can add to your bottom line, and if you hear of any others then grab those opportunities to learn with both hands.

PLANNING AND GOAL SETTING

Decide exactly what you want in your life right now. Visualise that there are no limits to your ability to achieve. Imagine that you have all of the time and money to do this. All of the friends and connections, all of the education and experience that you need to accomplish any goal you can set for yourself. Imagine that you could wave a magic wand and make your life perfect in the four key areas set out below.

INCOME	FAMILY
How much do you want to earn this year, next year and the year after?	What kind of lifestyle do you want to create for yourself and your family?
HEALTH	**NET WORTH**
How would this change your health and well-being?	How much asset or asset income do you want to have accumulated at the end of your career?

Goal Method – in forty seconds, write down four most important goals in life, do it now!

Write quickly. Whatever your answer is to this "Quick List System" way of writing goals, it is probably an accurate picture of what you really want.

Your goals must be in writing. They must be clear, specific, detailed and measurable. You must write out your goals as if you were placing an order to the universe. Make your description clear and detailed; don't say that you would like to handle a lot of money otherwise you may end up working as a bank cashier. Be more specific. Less than 3% of adults have written goals, or a plan, which is a big mistake. Get on the routine of planning and goal setting.

Set a deadline. Creating a deadline switches something on in your subconscious and drives you toward achieving your goals on time. If your goal is big enough, set steps. If you want to achieve financial independence, you may set a five or ten or even twenty year goal, and then break it down, year by year, so that you know how much you must save and invest each year.

Identify the hurdles that you will have to overcome to achieve your goal. Why aren't you achieving your goals, ask yourself lots of question to come up with the answers? What restrictions are in place that sets the speed at which you achieve your goal? The Pareto Principal, AKA the 80/20 Rule (a very interesting theory that I recommend you explore in greater detail) applies to restrictions. 80% of what is holding you back from achieving your goal is you! You may lack certain skills, education and experience all of which can be fixed.

Identify the knowledge, information and skills you will need to achieve your goal. Especially, identify the skills that you will have to develop to become the top in your field. Your skill sets the height of your income and your success. You can make more progress by going to work on the one skill that is holding you back more than any other this requires some personal development, which we cover later in the book. If you developed one skill and become the master this could have the greatest positive impact on your life? For example, I knew very little about tents until I set up Gala Tent. Now I'm an award-winning industry expert, set a goal to become an expert and to be the best.

Identify good people to add to your team to help you achieve your goal. Start with the members of your family, whose support you will require. I chose my brother-in-law and we still work great together twenty years on. Especially, identify the connections and customers whose support you will require to sell enough of your product or service to hit the targets you have set in your plan. Once you have figured out the people whose help you will require, ask yourself this question, "What's the value to them?" To achieve big goals, you need a lot of connections and a lot of clients.

Create a list. Let it consist of everything you will have to do to achieve your goal, and then combine the hurdles that you will have to overcome, the knowledge and skills you will have to develop, and the connections you will require. Plan every single step. As you think of new items, when you make out a list of all the things you will need to do to achieve your goal, you begin to see that this goal is far more achievable than you thought.

"A journey of a thousand miles begins with a single step." – **Lao Tzu.**

Organize your list into an action plan. You organize this list by arranging the steps that you have identified by priority. What do you have to do before you do something else, and in what order of Priority?

The 80/20 Rule says that 80% of your results will come from 20% of your activities.

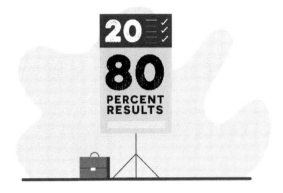

The 20/80 Rule says that the first 20% of time that you spend planning your goal and organizing your plan will be worth 80% of the time and effort required achieving the goal. So, you see planning is very important.

Make a plan

Organise your list into a series of steps from the beginning all the way through to the completion of your goal. When you have a Goal and a Plan, you increase the likelihood of achieving them. Plan each day, week or month in advance.

- Plan each month at the beginning of the month.
- Plan each week the weekend before.
- Plan each day the evening before.

The more in depth you go when you plan your activities, the more you will accomplish in a shorter time. The rule is that each minute spent in planning saves ten minutes in execution. This means that you get a 1000% return on your investment of time in planning your days, weeks and months in advance. Select your number one, most important task for each day. Set priorities on your list using the 80/20 Rule. Ask yourself questions; this is the only way you will get answers. Your brain is super smart, more intelligent than any computer, so use it.

Ask yourself which of those things, if you could only complete one, is most imperative?

Whatever your answer to that question, put this at the top of your list and mark down as Number One. From the remaining six, ask yourself the same question and place your answer at Number Two, and so on, until you have your seven actions, organized in priority order.

Focus your concentration on keys to success. Finding that focus means that you are aware of exactly what it is that you want to accomplish, and concentration requires that you dedicate yourself to doing only those things that move you toward your goals. I make a list every day and a list before I leave work for the following day. The un-subconscious mind is more powerful than the conscious mind so over night the tasks the next day become a lot easier as your mind has worked them out in advance. Sometimes I have completed my tasks before lunch, and I leave work early and get home to the family, which is also a very important job.

Develop the habit of self-discipline. Know what is most important to you, and then concentrate single-mindedly on that one task until it is 100% complete. This is not as easy as it sounds, as there is always a distraction. I have a discovery room at work, which I lock myself in either alone or with my team, if I only have one thing to concentrate on and I know the task is four to eight hours' work. This means that when I start with the task, I avoid all distractions and stay with that task until it is done.

Practice visualising your goals; create emotional pictures of your goals as if they were already a reality. See your goal as though it was already achieved, and you are simply taking steps towards it. Imagine yourself enjoying the success of this goal. If it is a fleet of luxury vehicles, imagine yourself driving one of them. If it is a holiday, see yourself on the beach sipping cocktails. If it is a new home that you want, see yourself living in a luxury new home. In visualising, take a few moments to create the emotions that would accompany the successful achievement. A mental image when combined with an emotion has a huge impact on your subconscious mind.

Visualisation is perhaps the most powerful preparation available to you to help you achieve your goals faster than you ever thought possible. When you use a combination of clear goals, combined with visualisation and emotional attachment, you activate your superconscious mind. Your superconscious mind then solves every problem on the way to your goal and activates the Law of Attraction, which begins to attract people into your life, as well as ideas and resources that will help you to reach those objectives quicker than ever.

"Was that a coincidence or did I make that happen?" – **Jason Mace.**

This is the explanation that I give to the law of attraction. And yes, I did say that, and I will say it again. The law of attraction is real. Things have happened in my business journey that I can't explain. Some people call this luck, but believe me you can make your own luck when you plan and take action. You only get out what you put in.

"You can't climb the Ladder of Success, with your hands in your pockets!" - **Arnold Schwarzenegger.**

Goal-Setting Exercise

Take a piece of paper, or pull up a word processing program, and place the word *Goals* at the top of the page along with today's date. Discipline yourself to write out at least ten goals that you would like to achieve in the next twelve months.

Begin each goal with *I*. Follow this with an action verb that is a command from your conscious mind to your subconscious mind.

Instead of writing in the future tense about what you *will* have, write is as though you have already achieved that aim. If your goal is to earn a certain amount of money in a certain year, you would say, "I earn £100,000 by the end of this year."

If what you covet is a new luxury vehicle, you would say, "I drive a Ferrari, or a McLaren by the time I am forty."

When you are documenting your objectives, always write them in the positive tense. Instead of saying, "I will quit drinking or smoking," you would say, "I don't smoke."

Always refer to your goals as though they were already a reality, as though you had already accomplished them. This activates your subconscious and superconscious minds to change your reality, so it is consistent with your commands.

Remember, your mind is a computer. If you say you can't, then this is an embedded command and you won't do it, and vice versa.

Decide upon your clear purpose. Once you have written out a list of ten goals, ask yourself this question, which all personal development coaches use, "If I could wave a magic wand and achieve any goal on this list, which one goal would have the greatest impact on my life or business, whichever your planning?"

Whatever your answer to that question, highlight that goal. Then, transfer the goal to the top of your list.

How to create your list

1. Write it down clearly and in detail.

2. Set a deadline on your goal and set sub deadlines if necessary.

3. Identify the hurdle that you will have to overcome to achieve your goal.

4. Identify the knowledge and skills you will need to achieve your goal, and the most important skill that you will have to study.

5. Identify the connections whose cooperation you will require and think about how you will bring them on board.

6. Make a list of everything you will have to do to achieve your goal.

7. Organise your list in order of priority.

8. Arrange your list into steps from the first to the last, with actions every day.

9. Plan your goal in terms of the activities that you will have to engage in to achieve it, daily, weekly and monthly, in advance.

10. Discipline yourself to concentrate single-mindedly on the most important thing that you can do today until it is 100% complete.

Make the conscious decision early on that no matter what occurs, you will never give up. Persistence is self-discipline in action. Each time you persist and overcome the failures and disappointments you will experience, you become stronger and better. You develop stronger and deeper character. You increase your self-esteem and self-confidence.

Your goal is to eventually become unstoppable and to never give up. Decide exactly what you want, write it down and plan and work on it every single day. By repeating the above steps until they eventually become a habit, you will find that you accomplish much more in the near future that many others cannot even dream of achieving in many years.

Start Now!

CREATE YOUR STARTER PLAN

Once you have conditioned yourself mentally, you'll think about the logistics of launching your brand new event industry venture. It is important to know how you intend to approach your business start-up.

Think about who you will target, and why. Think about your pricing structures, and how many of which jobs you'll need to take to pay for your goods, your time, and ultimately your bills.

You'll find a great example of a Marquee Hire plan over the page.

VALUE

A local Garden Marquee hire business where customers can call, book online a hire service and request a site survey.

VISION

To provide a unique affordable local Garden Marquee hire service specialising in the event industry, where the general public and businesses can hire marquees and gazebos along with accessories and props to host outdoor events secure and safe from the elements.

CURRENT **REALITY**

There is no local company providing a garden marquee hire service, which has created a unique opportunity for a new business start-up.

CURRENT CHALLENGE

To register a company name and URL domain name targeted locally, i.e. Marqueehireessex.co.uk. To create a website targeted at local business through Google, Bing, Yahoo, Scoot, Yell etc. This will rank us on online search tools, as well as creating free leads in our postcode areas. Create awareness through local press by working with local newspaper journalists providing stories of events around the area.

39

WHY WOULD BUSINESSES USE THIS SERVICE?

Local businesses will use this service for open days and corporate events, providing cover for their visitors and potential clients. Councils are always hosting events in the town and procure jobs for marquee hire so they are covered from the unpredictable weather.

WHY WOULD THE GENERAL PUBLIC USE THIS SERVICE?

Wedding, birthdays, anniversaries, family gatherings, hosting a garden party, Christmas or New Year's celebrations, there is a huge market for this service as the majority of people want the convenience of a third party coming to the home erecting a marquee and then taking this away after the event is finished.

PLANNING

- To Invest in stock
- To invest in a website
- List on all free local directories
- Set up social media profiles on: Facebook, Twitter, LinkedIn, YouTube, Instagram

INCOME I WILL GENERATE

1st Year £35,000 – £40,000

2nd Year £70,000 – £80,000

3rd Year £120,000+

PAYMENTS OPTIONS

30% deposit to save the day

Remittance balance 7 days before
the date of the event

Or payment in full on the booking day

POSSIBLE **PARTNERSHIPS** WHERE I CAN GENERATE INCOME

Mobile disco
Catering Companies
Fairground equipment
Toilet hire
Ice cream vendors
Children's entertainment
Props companies
Mobile big screen TV suppliers
Live entertainment events

TEN COMMITMENTS TO ACHIEVING SUCCESS

1. Action – you can have the best idea in the world, but if you don't put it in to action it will stay an idea.

2. Have Confidence in Your Ability - Trust that you are smart enough, and delete fear or doubt – these are the enemy. Trust in your abilities, as you are the same as anyone else; if they can do it, so can you.

3. Make it Happen – Discover a way of doing something different – and make it happen!

4. Work Smarter, Not Harder – Put systems in place that will do the hard work for you; clever systems are the difference between making a good company and making a great company. If you can spot a better way of doing something, then make sure you put it in place – and fast.

5. Think Big – Even when you feel small, think big. Visualise being the best at what you do.

6. Have an 'I Can' Attitude – Delete the words 'I can't' from your vocabulary. Replace instead with 'I Can', or 'I Must'.

7. Make Decisions - Don't be afraid to make decisions, just make fewer bad ones than good ones. Made a bad decision? Call it Research & Development and move on!

8. Learn – Work hard to defend and improve your business, as there's always a competitor trying to take it.

9. Charm - If you need to raise any concerns then always be charming, whether with a supplier, a customer or a work colleague. Add some humour where acceptable; this will diffuse any situation and get results, hopefully in your favour. Walk with your head held high, hold a good posture, and always look people in the eye. Honesty, a smile, nod or a wink, and good manners cost nothing. They go a long way, though, especially in business.

10. Give Back – Lend a hand and give back to your community by seeking out local projects that will add value to the company.

QUICK RETURN ON INVESTMENT

My company Gala Tent Ltd is looking to expand its distributor/installer network across the UK, Europe, and the Rest of the World, creating opportunities for people looking to set up their own marquee hire business.

With the majority of our marquee hire businesses being based in the South, there are huge opportunities for entrepreneurs looking to help set up more new businesses to serve the North of England as demand for hired marquees and gazebos from householders continues to soar.

Over the past twenty years, Gala Tent has helped dozens of dynamic individuals to take advantage of new business opportunities, many of which have been inspired to do so after buying a Gala Tent gazebo or marquee for an event.

Enterprising people interested in reaping the benefits of being a Gala Tent hire business will receive valuable support from the company; there is a great opportunity for new and established businesses to become part of our national hire network.

Whether you see this as a part time job to enhance your income, a full time career or if you want to add marquee hire onto an existing business, we can provide you with all the help and support you need. Gala Tent hire companies are experiencing significant growth in many market areas, such as garden parties and weddings, which offer great growth potential to independent businesses.

We provide Gala Tent hire companies with a high level of support and with low initial start-up costs and a quick return on investment, this can mean your business can be up and running and generating a profit in just a few weeks. You don't even need experience in the events industry, as this type of work suits anyone with drive and determination who wants to take advantage of a growing lucrative income stream.

Justin Harris, Managing Director of **Garden Party Hire**, based in Nottingham, said: *"My business has really taken off and we have a full order book, with many clients rebooking for next year too. We convert on average 93% of enquiries and gain most of our business from word of mouth. Summer and Christmas are our most profitable busy times. The reason for our success is we give people an event to remember at an unrivalled price and with impeccable service on top – what more could they ask for?"*

EVENT INDUSTRY ADVICE

When I get asked about what I do, and I respond that I work in the events industry, I always get a positive response. People have grand visions of me visiting exclusive venues, sipping champagne from flutes, attending awards ceremonies and eating canapés all day. Whilst that may be true some of the time, other times it's all about product development deadlines, managing projects and maintaining professional relationships.

However, it is the hire guys that get all the action. Some of our clients have amazing stories when I meet them at shows or at the Gala HQ. David Beckham, Marco Pierre White, Liz Hurley and Boris Becker are just some celebrity clients from our hire network so this job can be pretty cool! I myself have had an invitation to the House of Lords and a Royal invitation to Buckingham Palace, which I'm quite sure would not have occurred unless I was on the event industry boss journey. So, whether you've just hopped onto the career ladder and are hoping to get into the events industry, or you're currently employed but fancy a career change, this section will hopefully be of use.

Without a doubt, the events industry is a fun sector to work in, as it's dynamic and people-focused. It's an industry that is all about organisation, maintaining good relationships and being proactive. It's also an industry that tests your ability to think and solve issues creatively. It's also important to be up-to-date on industry news as there's always some new product or service trend that you could offer your existing clients to generate more income.

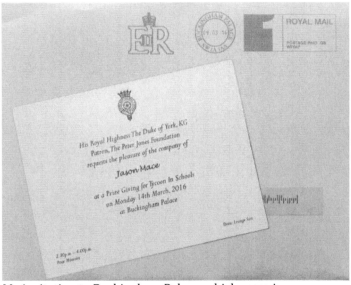

My invitation to Buckingham Palace, which came in recognition of my work with Dragon's Den's Peter Jones and his charitable foundation.

The events industry is a vast and ever-changing landscape, so if you plan to make your mark then you need to know where to aim for. There are so many different types of events; corporate events, weddings, music festivals, charity, press launches, conferences, industry exhibitions, the list goes on.

However as a start-up we recommend you start small with organic growth to bigger events, so stay local to begin with and target events such as garden parties, family events and your local council. When you have mastered your processes and understand how your business is going to run, then look further afield to build on your empire.

MARQUEE AND EVENT HIRING – THE BASICS

Pricing

The goal in pricing a service is to mark up your labour and material costs sufficiently to cover overhead expenses and generate an acceptable profit. First-time business owners often fail because they unknowingly price their services too low. According to industry expert (me, of course), fees are typically determined by three factors:

1. The Market Segment You Are Serving

Social events can have a different fee structure than corporate events. In the social events industry, hirers typically receive a fee for their services, plus if they've organised it, they can receive a percentage of some or all vendor fees. These two income streams produce enough revenue for a profit.

In the corporate events industry, however, event planners and hirers typically charge a fee for their services, plus a handling charge for each item they contract. For example, a hirer might buy decorative flowers from a

50

florist, marks them up (usually 15%) and charges that amount to the client.

Another possibility is a flat fee, or "project fee," often used when the event is large and the corporation wants to be given a "not to exceed" figure.

2. Geographical Location

Fees are higher in the South of England than they are in the North of England and Scotland. This difference reflects the cost of living. In addition, areas of the country that have well-defined on-and-off seasons base their prices partly on which season they're in. For example, in August in the height of Summer your services will be more in demand so you can be firmer about your price than in the cold winter months of January and February.

3. The Experience & Reputation of the Marquee Hirer

If you're just starting out in the industry, it's reasonable to charge less for your planning services as you gain expertise, increasing costs as the service received by the end user is inevitably bettered as you improve your skills and knowledge.

How, you may ask, are the above-mentioned fees-for-service calculated? Event planners price their fees-for-service (the total cost to the client) using a "cost-plus" method. If they need to contract out the labour, supplies and materials involved in producing an event, they will charge their clients a service fee of about 10-20% of the total cost of the event, with 15% being a rough average.

Coordination

After you've made the initial plans, your goal is to ensure that everyone is on the same wavelength. Good communication skills are important. Make sure any other vendors have at least a general idea of the overall event schedule. Even more important, vendors should be clear about what's expected of them, and when. Vendor arrival times should appear in the contracts, but verify those times anyway. This is a "check and recheck" period. Make sure all your staff members know their roles.

Patents and Trademarks

Entrepreneurs need to be aware of the importance of intellectual property when starting a new business venture. Whether you have developed an original product or designed an eye-catching company logo it is essential that you familiarise yourself with IP law. From information on patents and patent costs to trademarks and copyright this website on IP is an essential read for those starting a new business; www.ipo.gov.uk

OPERATIONS

Few, if any, event planners and hirers have nine to five jobs. Event planning often involves evenings, weekends, holidays and more often than not, seasonal peaks and troughs. How much time you must commit to working will depend, once again, on the specialist sector you choose to target.

Here are the main tasks you'll be completing as an event planner and hirer:

- *Research.* The best way to reduce risk (whatever the kind) is to do your homework. If you're new to the event planning industry, research may mean talking to other hirers who have produced events that are similar to the one on which you're working. Or it may be that you may find yourself reading up on issues of custom and etiquette, for example for a silver service party, especially if you're unfamiliar with that particular type of event. Whatever kind of event you're planning, research should include asking your client a lot of questions and writing down the answers to make sure you're both on the same page.

- *Design.* You may not be required to decorate and design the event, but if your clients ask then it's best to be prepared and offer this service. You will get an opportunity to let your creative side come out to play in the design phase of event planning, during which you sketch out the overall feel and look of the event. This is the time to work alongside your colleagues, employees or even simply sit by yourself, and brainstorm your ideas. It's also the time to pull out and look through your ideas file. (You do have one, don't you? If not, read on and take notes.)

Don't forget to consult your notes for the customer's answers to the questions you asked in the research phase. These responses, especially the one regarding the event budget, will help you thoroughly check each idea to ensure it is at all feasible, preferably before suggesting it to the client.

- *Form a Layout.* Once you've surveyed the site, spoke to the client and done some preliminary brainstorming, you should have enough information to form a layout. It's best to draw this so you have a visual for your team to look at and the client to feel comfortable.

- *Organisation.* Make sure you have a contact name and phone number (either the customer or someone acting on the customer's behalf) with whom you'll discuss all the important decisions. Having a designated contact helps guarantee that communications are easy.

- *Evaluation.* The true, and in one sense the most important, test of an event's success is customer satisfaction. The aim is to end up with a client who will sing your praises up and down the street, shouting it from rooftops. This is the client who will refer you to their family and friends, will hire you again, and who will provide word-of-mouth advertising for you.

There are many other ways to assess how successful an event has been; you can have a fellow event planner attend and scrutinise your event; plan a post-event dialogue with your workforce; acquire feedback from other industry professionals working at the event, such as the entertainers or the catering team; or survey guests at or after the event.

MARKETING IDEAS

Get your company listed in your local online directories, such as Yell, Scoot, or Yelp. You can add website address, photos and video content and its all FREE.

Google Business www.google.co.uk/business and www.bingplaces.com is another way for customers to find you online and is similar to Yellow Pages. So make sure to list your company on here, as this is also FREE.

Local free ad papers - if you are inventive with your ad, you can get free advertising from this avenue. These types of papers reach hundreds of potential clients; some also have an online presence and they are local so ideal for your start up business.

Get a website - just a homepage is enough to start with; you can request images from Gala Tent and a nice write up about you and your unique service. Register an email address to take booking inquiries. I would recommend using Gala Graphics to design you a bespoke website as they have done many others. Their work can be found at www.galagraphics.co.uk

Have some posters printed, put them in the window of local shops; ask friends and family to put your poster on their works' notice board. All this will cost you is the price of printing, so this is a very cheap way of getting your name out there.

Try some local leaflet drops; contact your local newspaper about adding your leaflet or flyer into the next weekly circulation, this method is extremely effective and very cheap.

Local radio can also be a good forum and can cost as little as £15 per airing, though you may have to pay around £100 for an advertising jingle.

Put a promotional offer in your local newspaper, as this can also be a good way to receive sales leads. Offer a free colour brochure (electronic or hard copy), as this will generate more enquiries and you will have something to follow up later.

Again, you can visit www.galagraphics.co.uk for help with leaflets and brochures.

Get listed with your local council as a supplier, councillors have large budgets for events in local communities and use a marquee hire and event services all year round.

Make contact with the large marquee companies in your area, inform them of your niche service which doesn't infringe on their market, they will be very happy to pass you the jobs they don't want or can't handle, and you will return the kind gesture.

Make partnerships with local DJs and Caterers, Hotels, as many of your parties will require this service, I'm sure they will pass your name on in return.

Hand your client a few leaflets after you have completed your hire job and ask them to pass your details on to friends and family. You will be surprised at how many booking you receive from referrals.

Monitor which ad source works best for you and follow the most productive avenue, immediately stop any advertising that doesn't produce leads.

Always store customer details (within the confines of GDPR regulations, of course) to mail with pre-booking offers, promotions etc. Join your local chamber of commerce and attend networking meeting to make valuable business connections. Chamber also host annual awards ceremonies so enter these when you have been established six months or more, as the local press is priceless and will look great on your website.

When you start up your business, write a press release. This is something that Gala Tent can help with, so email marketing@galatent.co.uk when you are ready for this service. Many of our start up businesses have won local awards for new business start-ups so make sure you're in your local awards category.

Use Social Media as much as you can. Facebook, Twitter, YouTube, Instagram and Pinterest are all good resources for news feeds, photos and videos etc. LinkedIn, for example has almost 33m active users, so don't underestimate the power of these tools, and best of all, they are largely FREE if you learn to use them wisely.

Customers need to see what you do, and an advertisement won't always accomplish that. I recommend networking and making friends in the industry. That way, people know you and trust you. They want honesty and integrity. Networking can help your business in two ways. If people have met you and know what services you offer, they may refer business to you or use your service themselves. Furthermore, networking with hotels, caterers and so on will give you a chance to meet some of the people whose services you may need as you plan events.

Although networking and word-of-mouth are the most common industry strategies for acquiring clients, traditional forms of advertising do have their uses. A new product or service card or brochure sent to a mailing list of prospective clients, or to local businesses may attract new business. A small ad in a local business magazine can help build name recognition. A Website may allow you to attract customers unresponsive to other forms of media.

PERSISTENCE PAYS

Ensure your marketing system involves relentless follow up. Not following up is one of the biggest marketing sins you can commit. Here are some statistics, which should scare the living daylights out of all of us!

48% of businesses never follow up with a prospect

25% of businesses make a second contact and stop

12% of businesses only make three contacts and stop

It's a staggering discovery, but only 10% of businesses make more than three contacts. It means they're losing a small fortune – and you could be too.

BECAUSE...

2%
of sales are made on
the first contact

3%
of sales are made on
the second contact

Not following up is one of the biggest marketing sins you can commit.

BECAUSE...

5%
of sales are made on
the **THIRD** contact

10%
of sales are made on
the **FOURTH** contact

80%
of sales are made on the
FIFTH to **TWELFTH** contact

So if you're like almost half of all businesses and make no more than one follow-up to your prospects... you're leaving 98% of your income on the table for someone else to come along and pick up. If that wasn't bad enough, here's why it's even worse than you think. Look at these eye-opening statistics about why people stop buying from businesses:

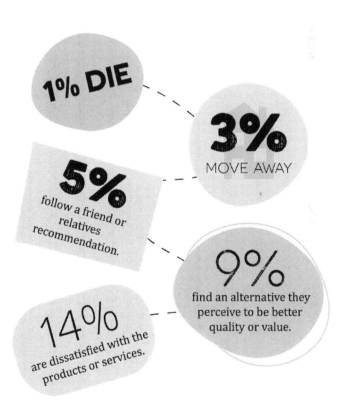

1% DIE

3% MOVE AWAY

5% follow a friend or relatives recommendation.

9% find an alternative they perceive to be better quality or value.

14% are dissatisfied with the products or services.

And a massive 68% of people leave a business because of... indifference. They take their business elsewhere simply because they do not feel valued.

So start courting your customers today!

BUILDING YOUR CLIENT DATABASE

The Key Points

- The more work you put in to your marketing mix ideas, the more results you will receive.

- Don't forget to store all your enquiry details, including name, address, phone, mobile number, and email.

- Always follow up a brochure request with a telephone call and ask for a booking.

- Do a site survey if necessary, which involves visiting the address of the potential client and measure the area to plan the event.

- People are creatures of habit and may book certain events every year so be sure to do your research.

Your customer database and potential customer database is the source of your trade. You need it to generate repeat business in the future, or as a fall back when times get tough and as an asset of your company when you want to exit. The most important thing, above all else, when compiling your database is include **everyone** that shows even a minute of interest in your company and what it is you do. Everyone that calls or meets you at a convention, venue or meeting is sent information - you should work towards improving and increasing entries. Without any clients your company is worth nothing - so don't neglect keeping records of the people you meet. Remember that it is the value or the information that you can collect.

The smallest and largest companies spend lots of money each year on their advertising to increase the amount of business they have. Often they don't always target new customers, but the existing clients that they have listed in their database. Keeping in contact with customers is a great way to get repeat business and promote new products to the right people. There are many different ways that you can maintain contact and interest with existing and potential customers, the most effective being email which is completely FREE.

With this in mind, make sure you keep in contact with your customers using emails on a regular basis, do an email campaign every week, or at a minimum of once a month. Make the content interesting; this could just be a case study from a recent job or some coverage in the press. The idea is use your email campaigns like social media posting interesting stories of events.

When emailing clients and prospects make sure you are following the new GDPR regulations and offer an opt-out option.

CONNECTING THE MARQUEE TO A HOUSE

I know of two sufficient ways to connect a marquee structure to a home or house. The first includes having the marquee right up next to the house so the guests walk straight in, the second requires a walkway between the two areas.

Attaching the Marquee to the House:

- This is usually done where there are doors from the house, so that they can use the end panels of the marquee as an entrance. This is a great choice for the English weather, as the water will run down the apex of the roof, past the sidewalls rather than the end panels. It's also handy for structural purposes as the framework is higher up at the end panels compared to the side panel areas, creating a more open, unobstructed entrance.

- The marquee should be right up to the house or building, as close as physically possible.

- Leave off the end panel facing the house and use it instead on either side of the marquee filling up any gap between the corners of the marquee and the house. This will also leave any windows in the house visible and looking in to the marquee, which will help the ambience of the event.

- A handy tip is to pull the scalloped edge of the canopy facing the house up slightly so it looks a little neater but also is able to aid keeping the heat in the marquee.

Using a walkway:

- It's easy to improvise and make your own walkway by using wood or PVC, and our Galatex is fantastic to use on hard surfaces and is non-slip.

- Remember to consider heating for your walkway if it's open to the elements.

- Try to keep the walkway a reasonably short length if the event is to be held in the house and the marquee, so people are encouraged to mingle between both, and neither is isolated.

The Gala Tent team are happy to offer custom advice for your events if needed. Just give us more info about the type of your event, the number of guests, any requested themes or special requests and we'd be happy to help.

LAYOUT ADVICE FOR THE MARQUEES

The easiest way to establish the size of marquee that you need is to first partition the marquee into areas. By partitioning the marquee you can begin to get an idea of the sort of space that you need to hold the guests that will be attending your event.

Our marquees' guideline capacity allows for approximately double the amount of people standing as it does for people seated with tables and chairs. This means that you can host double the amount of people for an event such as parties where people will be standing as you can for a sit down meal, for example, whilst still using the same size marquee.

The way that you layout your marquee is important to ensure that you optimise the room that you have available. For example if you are having a formal sit down meal it's important to use the main bulk of available room for table and chairs that guests can sit at, there would be no point using up room for a dance-floor etc, if nobody is going to use it.

So, add the following spaces together to get a good idea of the size of marquee any particular event would need.

Dining Area

If you are having a sit down event where food will be served it is important to organise your dining area and make sure that you have enough room for the amount of guests that would be attending.

As a rough guide for seating guests, we would recommend the following amount of people for each table size:

- 4ft round table – 4-6 people seated

- 6ft folding Granalite table – 6-8 people seated

- 8ft folding Granalite table – 8-10 people seated

The amount of tables that you wish to put in your marquee would depend on how much space you would like between the tables and how many guests you are expecting.

Reception Area

A reception area for your event is a great idea, it allows guests to have a space to chat and relax whilst getting to know each other. We would recommend a minimum space of 3m x 3m to comfortably accommodate standing guests. This area can also be used for guests to enjoy drinks and mingle away from the seating area.

Dancing Area

Gala Tent marquees are made up of 2m bays, which can be added or removed to change the marquee's size. We recommend around two bays for the dance floor depending on how many guests you are expecting. This allows enough room for your guests to dance and enjoy your event.

If for example you were hiring to an event for forty people seated you would need four 8ft folding trestle tables, or six 6ft tables. This would provide enough seating for all of your client's guests to be comfortable. We recommend a space of 4m per 8ft table, which means ideally you would need a marquee length of 8m to fit four tables.

You would also need to allow a minimum of one 2m bay for the reception area for guests to enter, stand and mingle. By adding together all of the space used by each area you can work out that a 6m x 12m marquee would be recommended.

Obviously, this is only a guideline and you may be able to use a smaller marquee or a larger one, should your client wish to give their guests a little bit of elbow room.

MARQUEE DÉCOR TIPS

Most people think a marquee is just a big tent, but they couldn't be more wrong! In its simplest terms, a marquee is a blank canvas, which can be easily transformed to suit any type of event, whether it is a wedding, a corporate event or a birthday party. You have all the freedom with the décor, and this allows you to explore your creativity. Even the plainest of marquees can be transformed into something completely magical with the right decoration. Here are some tips on how to make the marquee that you've hired out beautiful, and for further handy hints and tips, the Event Industry Experts from Gala Tent Ltd are always happy to help!

Tent lining

Wedding tents can be fully lined to create a cosy atmosphere and unique space. We sell satin lining and they can make a lot of difference to the look and mood of the space! If you are after a different style, lots of other companies hire them out separately.

This satin style of lining combines beautifully with both elaborate and decadent furniture, or with a simpler style for a country feel.

To avoid having to decorate the entire tent, plan for a "chill out area", this will make excellent use of some of the space. It's practical for the guests, who will appreciate an alternative space to sit down, chat, and relax instead of going back to their tables. It takes away the need to decorate this part of the tent – all that's needed is some furniture for the guests! Think couches, pillows, and a few flowers on side tables, and you're done!

Alternatively, you can achieve great results by twisting some choice fabrics around the poles, and letting them hang alongside the top of the tent. Make note of the ceiling – if you fancy birdcages for your centrepieces, you can economise by hanging a few from the top of the tent, instead of putting one on each table. You may also use hanging plants, or more fabric gathered at the top and hanging down in short garlands.

Real blooms

If you don't quite fancy draping fabrics around the marquee, then another brilliant option is foliage – real or fake. It doesn't have to cover the whole tent – you don't want to make it look or feel like your valued clients are getting married in a botanical garden or that your party theme is Little Shop of Horrors! By knowing your tent layout and the placement of poles you'll be able to figure out a few strategic places for the plants and flowers.

Light it up

Fairy lights and lanterns go a long way to create the right look and our marquees and lining take on colour very well. Think of contrasts – if you have dark reception furniture or chill out area furniture, contrast it with white or pastel fairy lights and lanterns or very vibrant warm colours to create a perfect balanced look. For a reception with a strong colour theme, go for lights in the lesser colours – for example, if you're having blue with touches of ivory, go for soft white lights to compliment the ivory.

Whatever you choose for the marquee, the possibilities are endless and hopefully we've sparked your inspiration!

GIVE A MARQUEE WEDDING THE WOW FACTOR

If you're covering a marquee wedding, one of the biggest worries for couples is definitely how to decorate it. Marquees can look a bit empty until the tables are laid, the flowers and the props are in position and the wedding guests are present in their finery. Here are some suggestions and advice on some of the more popular ideas for decorating a marquee for a wedding.

Make sure to create an all-important chill-out area where guests can take a breather from the party and catch up with one another. You can do this in a quieter part of the marquee, which is sectioned off from the main area, in an adjoining section, or if it's sunny you can always take it outside. Comfortable and practical, they really add a sense of sophistication.

Nothing says special like a chilled glass of Champagne so keep it nice and cool with classic champagne buckets dotted around your bar and lounge areas.

Poser tables and bar stools are great to have as well, so guests can mingle near the bar and dance floor adding to that fabulous party atmosphere. Gala Tent are able to supply these items and they can be found on the accessories section of the website.

Don't forget the lighting for when the sun goes down. Lanterns create a great atmosphere outdoors and simple coloured lighting really makes the theme rock.

Banish the British climate in the evening by adding some of Gala Tent's Far Infrared Patio Heaters to keep guests enjoying the outdoors as long as possible.

Lighting is really important in a marquee. Most come with up-lighters but to create the atmosphere you desire, adding your own lighting is key. I love the Gala Tent globe light sets with their soft ambience, but fairy lights placed over the dance floor or added to the whole ceiling, create a delicate twinkling effect – very romantic.

If you don't feel you can pull off decorations yourself, or choose not to include this kind of service within your portfolio, it is a good idea to research and introduce yourself to wedding decorators who have props and decorations ready for the special occasion. Having skilled businesspeople whose specialities compliment your own will mean you aren't turning down good business, and the more referral business you send their way, the more likely it is that it will be reciprocated when they are approached by other prospective clients.

CUSTOMER SERVICE

Excellent customer service combined with an excellent product can and will create loyal customers for life; walking, talking advertisements who are willing to advocate your business to friends, family and colleagues. Providing this type of excellent customer service starts with a genuine desire to delight your customers, but you also must think beyond selling your products or services. You need to consider the overall experience your customers have when they visit your store or website, what they think and feel, and what you can do to constantly improve this experience. So, I recommend small change frequently, over time these small changes add up to huge improvements.

Here are ways you can learn more about your customers and start to create a pattern of excellent customer service in your business.

Staff Training

It's important to make sure all your employees, not just your customer service representatives, understand the way they should talk to, interact with, and problem-solve for customers. Provide staff training that gives your staff the tools they need to carry good customer service through the entire customer experience. At Gala Tent we have systems and manuals and service level agreements that do it all.

Dealing with customer concerns

Dealing with a customer service issue or concerns can often involve sometimes intense emotions, so it's important to make sure you and others you have handling your customer service tasks are always courteous and respectful. Never be overly emotional, and allow those personal feelings override your wish to see your customer walk away happy. Have scripts for concerns to bring the customer back on track weather valid or invalid complaints.

No one ever learned anything by talking,

so listen.

Listening to your customer is one of the simplest secrets of customer service. Listening instead of simply hearing what your customers will teach you more about your business. Pick out the areas where they are displeased, while listening to what they say to you directly and take notes.

Respond by Return

There may be nothing worse than not responding to a customer concern and we have all been there, and sometimes it's so simple to resolve an issue, or the concern maybe just to find out more about what you're selling. It's imperative that you respond quickly to all enquiries, even if it is only an acknowledgement to say you are looking into the issue and will be back in touch. Some response is always better than none, so the customer doesn't feel ignored, so have something automated.

Ask for Feedback and reviews

When you have done a great job resolving a customer service concern, ask for feedback and a review you may receive a surprise or two when you learn about your customers and their needs, by asking them what they think of your business, products, and services. You can use customer surveys, feedback forms and questionnaires, as well as established and trusted review platforms, but you can also make it a common practice to ask customers first-hand for feedback when they have completed their orders. At Gala Tent we ask three questions after the customer has placed an online order.

- Tell us what persuaded you to buy from us today?

- Was there anything that you didn't like about making this purchase?

- Would you recommend us to your friends, family or work colleagues?

And we get lots of gold nuggets where we can improve from this feedback.

Use Feedback You Receive

You need to act on the feedback you receive from customers in order to make it useful in your customer service process. Take time to regularly review feedback, identify areas for improvement, and make specific changes in your business.

Excellent customer service often comes down to consistently checking in with your customers and making sure they are happy with not only the products and services you're selling, but also the process of purchasing, ordering, working with you, etc. If you do that successfully, you are on your way to becoming known for providing and winning awards for your excellence in customer service.

Get Rid of Bad Business

Weed out bad customers. When you're trying to hold on to every last customer, you might not realise that some of them are doing your company more harm than good. One thing most business owners don't consider is whether their best business decision may actually involve stopping their account, or at a minimum stop the discount and credit.

What Makes A Bad Customer?

- Those who require a serious amount of maintenance.

- Those who are demanding or abusive to your staff.

- Constant complaints about your product or service when you have no doubt that it is fit for purpose.

- Return of product in serious high volume, reports missing items or is unhappy constantly.

- Constantly asking for replacement items or freebies

Here is some advice for how to handle your bad customers:

- Identify the real problem. Investigate if the problem rests with you ask other customers for feedback of the issues, which have been raised.

- Take responsibility. Show good faith to sort any problems if the complaint lies with you and has substance. This will salvage the relationship and give your customer confidence for future dealing.

- Present your issue. The customer might be receptive to your feedback, and they might provide a positive response that may turn things around making them a good customer again. Or they may not...

- Interview your staff; get feedback from your staff handling the account, this will prove positive in your final decision.

- Do your numbers. Do some number crunching and have serious look at the clients account, take in consideration labour, returns value the whole shebang, you may be surprised to find out the account is not profitable or even worse you maybe losing money?

- Establish a 'three strikes and you're out' policy. Obviously don't give the customer this information but internally train your staff to recognise this system.

- Tell the client your relationship has become strained and your product and service do not complement each other and not suitable. Refer them to another supplier or just recommend they source the service / product elsewhere thanking them for the business and wish them best of luck.

Losing any customer may cause a likely drop in turnover but on the positive side if the account was not profitable you'll free up resources to find and build more profitable business relationships, one-door closes another door may open.

THE IMPACT OF TESTIMONIALS

Testimonials are one of the most powerful marketing tools you'll ever have at your disposal and they're FREE.

What is a testimonial?

Testimonials are written or recorded statements by customers that support your credibility and level of expertise. They also strengthen your reputation by expressing the trust that other people have in you and what your business does. Testimonials are a fantastic tool with which you can attract a deeper interest from prospective clients and existing clients, which will ultimately make you and your business increasingly successful.

Why are they so powerful?

It's easy to say great things about yourself, anyone can do that. But with a testimonial, you've got someone else doing it. And bear in mind this is someone else the prospective client can identify with, simply because they are in the same position that the person giving the testimonial was in before they bought your product or service.

Now, one big advantage of having a testimonial on hand in the event industry is you have social proof that you deliver what you say. It's also a good idea to carry an iPad or tablet to show photos of successful jobs you've done, a picture is also a great testimonial to your work and paints a thousand words. Get them displayed on your website along with your testimonials.

You can also add more value with reviews on third party websites such as www.rivyoo.co.uk and Google My Business, which are both free. However, these are a little more difficult to acquire, as you will need to work hard on these because the client would need to sign up and give some personal info away. They are very valuable though, as you usually only read negative feedback on these kinds of review sites, so to have positive reviews on a third party website can have a very high value.

There's no doubt in my mind that videos sell better than any picture or text online so video some events as well. You will also be working mainly face-to- face with clients, and speaking to people at events where you are displaying your services makes it a lot easier to win business and this is a huge positive in the event industry.

HOW TO BUILD A BRAND

Building a trusted trademark brand from the ground up is no easy task.

"What should it look like?"
"How should it make people feel?"
"Will it get my message across to my target audience?"

These are questions that naturally come up when you start the discovery journey of how to connect the dots between which services you're offering or what you're selling and who it is that you're trying to reach.

Whether you've a start-up or looking to enhance your existing brand, here's everything you need to know about building a strong brand for your business.

What Exactly Is a Brand?

A brand isn't just a recognizable name and logo that distinguishes you in a crowded market.

Your brand is how people identify you. We all have a personal brand that means something different to everybody we meet. We each many different traits that leave different impressions on different people, and what they say about us when we're not there. So as an individual always leave a good impression and look after your personal brand on the way.

Likewise, businesses have names, products, logos, colours, fonts, a language, a mission statement, and most importantly a story that make up who they are and affect how they are identified.

For example, here is the Gala Tent logo – The colour blue represents trust, bank logos are all usually blue if you look at them, as they are the colour of trust. In our case we also want to project the outdoors and the blue sky. The text **GALA TENT** in capital letters in Gold represents the Gold customer service and quality of product that we supply. The logo breaks away in to lines, which represent a modular tent that you can add to. The shape is of a pitched roof, representing cover. The name Gala represents a social occasion with special entertainments or performances. We added the union jack to our logo a decade ago to promote our British authenticity along with a very clever marketing device, with the mission statement *Designed and Build in Britain*. This still works for us today, it's a great mission statement and one I am very proud of.

7 STEPS TO BUILDING YOUR BRAND...

1 Write your story first (very important, there'll be more on this in the next chapter)

2 Choose your business name.

3 Write down what you want to achieve

4 Research your target audience and your competition.

5 Write a good catchy marketing slogan (short and striking memorable phrase)

6 Choose the look of your brand (colours and font).

7 Design your logo.

Let's start with laying the groundwork to inform the way you go about building your brand.

Figure Out Your Place in the Market

Before you start making any decisions about your brand, you need to understand the current market: who your potential customers and current competitors are.

There are many ways to do this:

- Google your product or service category to view your competition

- Check out your competition reviews, to get a feel for what their clients are saying about them. Negative reviews can be gold nuggets in a prospective client's decision making process.

- Chat to people who are part of your target market and ask them which services/product they buy in your space.

- Twitter, Facebook, or LinkedIn are good for this, as you can run a campaign and target your audience.

- Look at groups and pages on social media that your target audience follows and are receptive to.

- Go shopping online or offline and get a feel for how your customers would browse and buy service / products.

As you go about your research, make a note in your journal. If you don't have a journal then I suggest you immediately invest in one. I had a Filofax in my early days in business, and I still have it now to reflect back on. I also had a small notebook and I never left the house without it. Today my mobile phone notebook is crammed with notes I make almost every day. I even wrote the note of writing the workshop to help our client base and add value. If our clients are doing well then so are we.

Who are your lowest hanging fruit customers?

These are the ones that you can easily sell to.

Who are your top 3 competitors?

Think about the brands that are established and known in the market.
Where do your customer chat and what are they chatting about? You want to know their

interests, so check out forums in your field and actively listen to your prospective clients' interests and fears.

What is your ideal client, and who do you want to work with?

Find your ideal demographic and set the bar high.

It's important to have this knowledge before moving forward with your business plan as it will inform you about what your brand should focus on and how it can position itself apart from the competitors.

Define Your Brand's Focus on Value

It's important to focus on value. It's all about value. Let that form all the other parts of your business and brand as you build it. If you add value to someone life, then you have a great brand.

Here are some questions and exercises to get the juices flowing.

What's your Mission Statement?

A Mission Statement, in my opinion, is a snappy line that stakes your claim to your portion of the market.

Take SOTpay, for example, which is the flagship product of my Gala Technology business. Its Mission Statement strapline is SECURE. COMPLY. PROTECT. Three simple words that say it all.

SECURE the transaction and your money
COMPLY: Simplified PCI DSS Compliance
PROTECT your business

It's simple, and it's incredibly effective.

Your USP (or unique selling point) is the one thing you're competing on. Find it, go in on it, and make it a part of your brand's messaging. Alternatively, if the company you want to start has a cause at its core (e.g. if you're starting a social enterprise or charity), you can also write this out as a mission statement that makes a clear promise to your customers or to the world. For example, I will not fiddle the money people send and donate for charity, probably not the best line but you know where I'm going with that with my trust and value strategy.

Which words work with your brand?

One way to look at your brand is as if it's you. What would you like? What kind of value would you require being the client? For me it was delivery, when I wanted to find a Marquee delivered next day for the Millennium celebrations. I added to my business model later and made delivery free, which was a huge hit with my client base and still is. What I do has been imitated many times, but the copy cats simply don't deliver the value, quality, or service that Gala Tent achieves. Most of the times that a client has purchased from elsewhere, they have been seduced by a cheaper price, which comes at a cost, but inevitably they always come back to Gala Tent.

We over deliver in all areas and then they get it, they see the value. You should take on the same model. You can manufacture anything cheaper and you can offer a cheaper service, but do expect to provide a lower quality product or job. But it's not just the price of the product. Think about back up service, maintenance, or spare parts. All of these add value, which come at a cost so never undersell yourself.

What you are doing is asking yourself questions, which is the only way you will come up with answers. If you are struggling, get a team of trusted friends or colleagues together and throw some questions in the mix. A white board works well in this format. If you don't have a white board then take notes in the journal you've now purchased.

A fun and useful branding exercise is to pitch 3-5 adjectives that describe the type of brand that might click with your audience.

What metaphors or concepts describe your brand?

Thinking about your brand as a metaphor or conceptual characteristics can help you to identify the individual qualities you want it to have.

This can be a vehicle, an animal, a celebrity, a sports team, anything. If it has a prominent reputation in your mind, it will summon the sort of vibe you want your brand to give off. For example, if I wanted to create a brand targeting entrepreneurs, I might choose to use the cockroach as a starting point; they're super survivors that will do anything to thrive and will still be around even after a nuclear blast. I have no problem identifying with these creatures, as they can adapt to any environment, which is the kind of trait that will set you apart from others as they fall by the wayside. So, if your brand was a creature, what would it be and why?

Here's another exercise that might help you to rid yourself of any mental blockers when working on your brand. Someone must chair this and everybody needs a pen and paper at least, but it does work better with white board for a group brainstorming session. You can draw a few doodles on paper and do hand outs and ask everyone to write
the answers down for a big reveal at the end.

1st Exercise
So, you inform the players that there is a 3ft high bar in front of them. How do they get over this? You cannot go around this or under it, write 3 answers down.

2nd Exercise
The bar has now been raised to 6ft you still cannot go around it or under it, but you have to get over it. Write 3 answers down.

3rd Exercise
The bar is now raised to 100ft how do you get over this? You still cannot go around it or under it but you must get over it. Write 3 answers down.

Now this is where it gets really interesting. You really don't have to be very creative to work out how to get over a 3ft or 6ft hurdle, but 100ft hurdle forces creativity, and you will be amazed at some the answers.

So, promise me you will set the bar high you will be surprised with what you can achieve.

I started with a £2000 credit card investment, that's really no money at all in the grand scheme, and now I have a multi-million pound operation. I own restaurants, wedding venues, commercial buildings, patents and trademarks. My company invented the SOTpay technology, which is another story for another time, but the point is that I am no smarter than you are, I just set the bar high.

Choose a Business Name

Choosing my first business name was a total flop. I remember I didn't put any thought in at all. I was making money and I went to the bank to set up a business account. The manager asked me my business name. I told him that I hadn't even thought of that, so I just said Jason Mace. So, my first business account was, yes, Jason Mace Business. When I see companies now with a name like John Lewis or Paul Smith, then I'm sure they did the same thing, right?

What's in a name? Depending on the kind of business you want to start, you can make the case that your name matters very little or it matters a lot. In my opinion, it needs to reflect what you are selling or what service you are offering, so don't over complicate it.

As a business owner, your company's name is probably one of the first big commitments you must make. It'll impact your logo, your domain name, your marketing, and trademark registration (which I would also recommend if you are going through all the discovery process).

Here's a useful link to register your trademark **https://www.gov.uk/how-to-register-a-trade-mark** - only use .gov websites as there are some unscrupulous sharks out there that will charge you £1000, for what should cost around £200 if you do it yourself online. As an unstoppable entrepreneur, I do this a lot, and it's easy.

Ideally, you want a business name that is difficult to copy. You can back this up by registering the word i.e. Gala Tent. I own the term Gala Tent, so our competitors can't use this (although they have tried, and I have spanked them royally, so it pays to trademark). You should do the same., and protect what you intend to build.

Do some Google searches for names, and be sure to check you can buy the domain name as well. Brainstorm some names, or try one (or a combination) of the following approaches:

- You could be very brave and make up a word like Pepsi, but then again, it's not that brave as they ended with **Pepsi Cola**.

- Use a suggestive word or metaphor or simile.

- Describe it literally, like Marquee Company (not very creative or sexy but it says what it is)

- I like Hindu words; Marquee is Maarkee. This kind of thing can only enhance your story.

- Create a portmanteau word, which is a made-up amalgamation of two existing words. Pinterest (pin interest), for example.

- Use the initials of a longer name, like YBBC (Yorkshire Billionaires Boys Club).

- Or just be super brave and creative, and invent a word?

Remember since your brand name will also affect the domain/URL of your website, be sure to shop around to see what's available before you decide.

Choose Your Brand's Colours and Fonts

Once you've got a name down, you'll need to think about how you'll visually represent your brand, namely your colours and typography. This will come in handy when you start to build your website.

Choosing Your Colours

Colours don't just define the look of your brand; they also convey the feeling you want to communicate and help you make it consistent across your entire brand. You'll want to choose colours that differentiate you from direct competitors to avoid confusing your target audience.

Some emotive words that are associated with particular colours that can assist with your decision are below, including existing brands that famously use those colours.

RED – Passion, exciting, bold, youthful, energetic, ambition, confidence
Brands – Kelloggs, Coca Cola, Lego, Virgin

PINK – love, calm, warmth, assertive, intuitive, respect
Brands – Barbie, Cosmopolitan, T-Mobile

PURPLE – Creativity, compassion, individual, wealth, original, distinguished
Brands – Cadbury, Yahoo, Milka, Hallmark

NAVY – Loyalty, sincere, authority, peace, control, success, responsible, communication
Brands – Facebook, Reebok, Twitter, Gap

GREEN – Balance, growth, restore, equilibrium, generous, clarity
Brands – BP, Body Shop, Starbucks, Asda

BLUE – Spirit, perspective, content, ambition, goals, self-sufficient, aware
Brands – Ford, Amex, PayPal

ORANGE – Instinct, optimistic, extrovert, freedom, impulse, motivation
Brands – Fanta, Penguin Books, Mastercard

Colour psychology isn't an exact science, but it does help to inform the choices you make, especially when it comes to the colour you choose for your logo.

Choosing Your Fonts

At this point, it's also good to look at fonts you might want to use on your website.
Pick three fonts, one for headings and one for body text one for your logo. The typography of your content should be clear, easy to read, and if you can help it, specific to you and your brand.

Write a Slogan

A catchy slogan can often be a very valuable asset, something brief and descriptive that you can put in your Twitter bio, website headline, business card, and anywhere else where you've got very few words to make a big impact.

Keep in mind that you can always change your slogan as you find new angles for marketing your products or services. Gala Tent has three main slogans, of which at least one will feature in everything that we do.

- It's not an event without Gala Tent
- Your event covered, next day
- Designed and Built in Britain

Designed And Built In Britain

Slogans are easy to come up with when you have millions of pounds in your marketing budget to enforce them. Take a look below at these short slogans from the big boys. They make a strong impression, and this will give you some ideas to approach writing a slogan of your own:

Adidas – "Impossible is nothing"
Apple - "Think different"
Carlsberg - "Probably the best lager in the world"
Nike - Just do it"
Red Bull - "Red Bull gives you wings"
KFC - "Finger Lickin' Good"
Subway - "Eat Fresh"
Kit Kat - "Have a Break, Have a Kit Kat"
Heinz - "Beanz Meanz Heinz"
Skittles - "Taste the Rainbow"
Rice Krispies - "Snap! Crackle! Pop!"

Try www.slogangenerator.org to brainstorm some ideas. It may help you to create something special. Good luck!

Design Your Logo

A logo is probably one of the first things that come to mind when you think about building a brand. This is for good reason. It's the face of your company after all, and could potentially be everywhere that your brand exists.

Ideally, you'll want a logo that's unique, identifiable, and that's scalable to work at all sizes (which is often overlooked).

Consider *all* the places where your brand's logo needs to exist, from your website to your Facebook Business profile picture, to the thumbnail you see in browsers and apps. If you have a logo as your Instagram profile image that is 90% text, for example, it'll be almost impossible to read.

Get a square version of your logo created, one that has an icon element that remains recognizable even at smaller sizes.

Research how some of the big brands do this, as it is very smart and they will have paid hundreds of thousands for this creative thought process, and you can view this for free, but don't copy just model yours around this.

An abstract logo has no explicit meaning. It's just a shape and colours that you can't easily tie back to anything in the real world.

I'm not a fan of abstract logo as for me they don't get the message across. They force you to spend budget on getting this kind of a logo over the line and embedded in your prospective clients' minds. But this isn't to say they don't have their place in business. Abstract logos have no innate meaning to anybody except their creator, until they become synonymous with the brand they represent. They may suit your business model and what you want to achieve, so it's a decision that only you can make. If you do this, I'd be interested in knowing how you get on.

Mascot logos are often represented by the face of a character. For example in gaming, something like a wolf, a skull, or a dragon. This may help to humanize or animalise the brand.

Emblem logos, think about brands such as Harley Division, Porsche, Costa Coffee, often combining text with an emblem for a bold and regal look, these make very recognisable and memorable logos and one which can work really well, especially as illustrated by the aforementioned very successful names.

Letter mark logos, think CNN, JVC, IBM, turn the initials of your full business name into a logo. If you chose a business name with three or more words, this might be a style you'd want to consider, especially if the initialism creates a catchy and original acronym.

An icon logo, think WhatsApp, Instagram, Facebook is your brand represented as a visual metaphor. Unlike an abstract logo, an icon logo suggests something about the product (Twitter's bird is suggestive of the frequent short "tweets" on the platform).

Word Mark logos, think Google, eBay, FedEx. Turn your brand name, colours, and font into a visual identity. The problem with word marks is that they're often hard to create a square design for social media platforms, but Facebook have managed to achieve this by simply using the first letter, and that **F** has become easily one of the most instantly recognisable images in the constantly online world we live in.

Consider McDonald's for a minute. Because of the limitations that exist for each logo type, many logos are a combination of styles. If you are a new business, and you don't need to choose an icon over a wordmark when you can get the best of both. This makes it easier to satisfy the condition of creating a scalable logo while still putting your brand name front and centre. McDonalds, for example, can use their iconic golden arches wherever the full wordmark doesn't fit.

Unless you've got design of your own, you may need some help. Of course, I have a ready made solution in my print and design company, Gala Graphics, and we can also provide you with all your brand guidelines, which can then be used for business cards flyers and brochures. Gala Graphics design team can also create your website around your logo, so take some action and get a quote.

Extend your brand throughout your company

Building a brand doesn't stop with creating a logo or slogan. Your brand needs to be consistent, wherever your customers interact with you, from the theme you choose for your website to the marketing to customer service to the way you package and ship your products. Basically splatter your logo everywhere! There is no such thing as too much brand awareness. You'll continue to shape and evolve your brand as you expose more customers to it

Marketing your business

Marketing done right can generate incredible returns on investment for your business. Done wrong, however, it can feel like throwing money down the drain, or one of my favourite slogans, kicking money into the grass. Because small business owners or mindful of cash flow all the time, there is a need for creativity all the time. It can be difficult to master all the different levels that go into sales or marketing. If the prospect of actively chasing sales is something that fills you with dread, fear not. The following workshop marketing tips for start-ups will help you win more sales, market your product or service better and waste less money.

Sell the benefits, not a comparison

How you market yourself is all about highlighting what makes you different. There are four major ways to do that.

> - Your offer adds more value
>
> - Your quality for exceeds your competitor
>
> - Your back up and customer service is exceptional
>
> - Your guarantee surpasses your rival.

But how you sell yourself is different than how you *market* yourself. You can tell someone that you provide a product or service that is cheaper or more effective than that of another business, but that doesn't say how much more value you are going to add the customer's life or business.

Selling is about the benefit. A comparison may highlight the features you offer, but you are always selling value and benefits.

Listen to your customer

Sam Walton of the huge organisation WalMart started his empire in rural America. This was despite the existing business logic saying a mass retailer anywhere but in a city with a concentrated population would fail. The logic was, if you wanted to move mass quantities of goods, you needed mass quantities of people.

But Walton knew his customers because he would frequently listen to them first-hand. He was aware that people who lived in rural and suburban areas often bought in larger quantities because they had larger families or needed more goods to keep their own small businesses stocked and running. Walton listened to his customers, and the result is the largest, most powerful brick and mortar retailer in the world. The customer may at times defy logic, but they are always right, so listening to their feedback carries benefits to you. The Gala Tent product range evolved from customer feedback, so I know first hand that this is powerful stuff.

Walton also over took many of his competitors as he was a pioneer in operating systems, and his competition could not keep up. At this point, I would like to emphasise the importance of systems and automation. Large companies these days are like steering the Titanic and decision-making is sometimes nigh on impossible, because the road map is backed up due to dated and unmanageable systems. Therefore, it's quite easy for them to be disrupted by a slicker more agile newcomer to the market, so keep your systems up-to-date constantly improving them and you will thrive. A huge part of Gala Tent's success is down to systems. From Day One I always invested in developing systems, and as a result we are always a dot on the horizon to our competitors.

Market your product before it's ready

Some businesses wait until their product is perfect before they do any marketing or awareness campaigns. That can waste valuable time which you cannot afford at this crucial time of your business journey. Many businesses expect to sell their product as soon as it's ready. But if no one knows about it, then demand will start at zero until you undergo a marketing campaign to build brand awareness for potential customers. Build a buzz ahead of time and you'll hit the ground running.

What we do at Gala Tent is create a listing and ask for pre orders, or gauge interest, and this is easy. You can also ask for pre orders of anything, and offer an incentive like a discount for waiting but being the first to have the new innovative product or service. This way you can sell the benefit of the product or service before it becomes available. This way, when the product is market ready, so are your customers!

Think outside the box

My team prefer the term **lateral thinking.** The marketing landscape has dramatically changed since I set up Gala Tent twenty years ago. Back then, there were no search engines or social media platforms. There was the Internet, but it was very much in its infancy and very few customers had email. Nothing was FREE. It was all paid advertisements. Now, start-ups have access to free, online marketing platforms. For example, you can use online YouTube video marketing, social media, blogs, competitions, content marketing, and podcasts.

Monitor your advertising

Marketing that you can't monitor is failed marketing, and leads to more kicking money into the grass. Sure, you may spend money to do some advertisement, and you may even see an uptake in sales around the same time you ran the ads. But how can you be sure what you spent on the ads relates to your new sales? Maybe it was something else altogether. Maybe there is a natural, seasonal uptake for what you sell that will go away in a month. This drives me crazy so monitor your advertising to see what works best for you.

If you're going to commit time and money to a marketing campaign, make sure you can measure the results. Set up ways to track conversions where you can insert code to your website and track where the traffic is coming from.

Track incoming calls and jot down where your customer has seen your advertisement, then add this information to your systems that stem from each marketing campaign. Also, run multiple types of marketing campaigns in distinct, small batches. This will allow you to compare marketing channels and see which perform best. Immediately weed out the ones that don't work and invest more in those that do.

Test multiple marketing channels

As mentioned above, it's good to test multiple marketing channels and ideas to see what works best. Often, it's not any one thing but a combination of all the above. When your customer hears you on the radio, sees you in a search engine result, and then finds you mentioned in a blog, YouTube video or Facebook ad, they start to accept your brand and subliminally store the story. They may not have the need for your product or service immediately, but when they do, it will be your name that comes to mind instead of a competitor's.

Add some PR and Social Proof to the mix

If I walk in to a room, or onto a stage and just blurt out how great I am, how great my company is, and how many awards I have won, those in attendance would only have my word to take on that, and treat my self-aggrandising with a pinch of salt. However, if I was introduced as a successful award-winning entrepreneur with an award-winning product and service which added value to the event industry, people would then clap and welcome what I had to say next. When you do traditional advertising, it's your marketing material selling your product. When you perform PR or have a member of the press or a media house that covers your industry talk about you, it's brand building and endorsement, which is much more powerful.

Here is some credibility building, if your company is featured in your high profile local or national press, you'd be silly not to put that paper's name on the front of your company's website? Even if your company was only mentioned by way of a quote, you are still "as mentioned in Financial Times or Sunday Times." When customers see that publication's name next to your company's name, it builds trust and credibility.

Even little PR wins add up to a greater sum of its parts. Local news or blogs, for example, can be invaluable to your company. And, unlike most traditional marketing, PR endures far beyond the dates of the advertising campaign. Good PR can do a lot for your credibility and brand awareness, and if you are only operating local to begin with, then this is easy as journalists are always looking for stories, and the story of a local person achieving success is always desirable. You're a son or daughter of your village, town or city. Your neighbours *want* to hear of your success, so tell them via a media that they trust.

Customer Feedback

There's a chapter on this later in the book, but good or bad, you want to know what your customers are saying about you. If you don't provide your customers with a place to complain or praise you, it makes it look like their thoughts and opinions don't matter. Remember, even if a customer comes to you and is furious, that's a great opportunity for you to publicly show how willing you are to right a wrong, or make a customer feel valued -- which is PR gold.

I recommend www.rivyoo.co.uk as a good place to start, and you've no doubt spotted it - RivYoo is the Hindu word for Review. This is a great review website designed by me and free for you to use. This is the only review centre where you can retain your client as there are special tools in the review management system.

Other review sites like TrustPilot or TripAdvisor have never historically offered this facility. They don't genuinely care if a competitor has used a "sock puppet" account to leave bad reviews and attempt to tarnish the reputation you've spent so long building up. This always annoyed me, so I built a better system. RivYoo is that system.

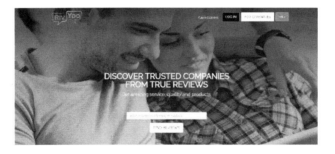

Our review software has a unique response management system should you receive a fatal bad review, helping you resolve a problem fast and retain your customers.

By providing a place on your site for this kind of exchange to happen, you can address the issue and control the customers concern. The alternative is that your customer goes to a third-party site and leaves a very damaging review where you can't address the issue, and in some cases being blackmailed.

Rewards and Retention schemes

Reward loyalty or interest. I tell my team at Gala Tent that our customers are our sales department. Word-of-mouth testimonials and customers who are brand advocates are better than any paid advertisement. So, I continuously reward customers with competitive pricing, incredible customer support and automatic updates to enhance their purchase. The next step is to actively assist in their business growth, offering workshop manuals as an additional service. At Gala Tent, the purchase is not the end of our client's journey with us. It's only the beginning. We take an active interest in how our clients use our products, and we look for ways to help to enhance their own business. Always give back.

THE IMPORTANCE OF HAVING A GREAT STORY

People buy into stories before they buy products. Today, every marketer understands that a good story has the potential to sell just about anything. But, still, few understand the right way to use story and narrative to guide people on the perfect journey.

This is due in large part to the fact that it takes some creativity and thought. We all have a story. You may think it's not interesting, but it is, and people want to hear it. A question that will crop up a lot for you as your success grows will be *Why did you start you own business?*

A great story has many significant elements and to have the greatest impact each part must be built in a certain order. Your story needs to match your work ethics, and be something that your client can relate to. Here are some great examples of how a story becomes an integral part of a brand, starting with that of the company that set me onto the path of success that I tread right now.

Gala Tent Ltd.

Gala Tent was established when I was working behind the bar of my parents' Working Men's Club in 1999, and the Millennium celebrations were fast approaching. I called around local and national companies in the yellow pages, looking to hire a marquee for the club's Millennium event. The response from every supplier was that they were fully booked. The lack of available tents was very disheartening at the time, but it provided me with a spark of an idea. If I couldn't get hold of a tent, then surely there were thousands more like me whose events would be going without too. So, armed with a credit card and an idea, I purchased some stock and set about finding willing buyers, of which there were enough to sustain the Gala Tent brand in its early years.

Since then, I have been innovating, investing in, and manufacturing a range of marquees and gazebos. It's this commitment to continuous improvement and staying one step ahead of the competition that has seen Gala Tent grow into the UK's number one supplier of event structures. The tents' versatility ensured that many different industries and sectors found them as an invaluable business investment. Gala Tent holds several million pounds of stock within its 60,000ft^2 Distribution Centre at any time, so next working day delivery can be as good as assured.

Now in its 20th year in business, Gala Tent is an award winning, market leading company, and the preferred contract supplier for many hire companies, councils and branches of the emergency services and the military. Gala Tent is trusted brand used by Virgin, Lego, RAC, RAF, high profile film productions, even Google and No 10 Downing Street purchase from Gala Tent.

I'm sure you will agree it's a great story and one I never get fed up of telling. When I am asked, and I am asked a lot, "How did you get in to selling marquees?" I have my story mapped out ready and it is always well received, especially as it offers hope to the ambitious, since I started the company on a £2000 credit card investment back in 1999 and have now evolved Gala Tent into a successful multi-million pound business with several offshoot brands and companies, each with rapidly growing success in their own fields.

Marks and Spencer

Marks & Spencer started life more than 130 years ago when the Jewish immigrant Michael Marks came to the north of England from his hometown of Slonim, Belarus. He arrived with little money and spoke poor English. Beginning as a peddler, he soon owned a market stall in Kirkgate Market in Leeds. He classified everything by price, but quickly stopped selling more expensive items when the penny section thrived with the slogan **'don't ask the price, it's a penny'**.

Michael decided to look for a partner to help manage his growing business. He initially approached Isaac Dewhirst, who had loaned money towards his original start-up costs. Isaac declined but recommended Tom Spencer – his senior cashier. Tom agreed, and on 28 September 1894 Marks & Spencer was born.

Coca Cola

John Pemberton, an Atlanta pharmacist, was inspired by simple curiosity. One afternoon, he stirred up a fragrant, caramel-coloured liquid and, when it was done, he carried it a few doors down to Jacobs' Pharmacy. Here, the mixture was combined with carbonated water and sampled by customers who all agreed this new drink was something special. So, Jacobs' Pharmacy put it on sale for five cents (about 3p) a glass. Pemberton's bookkeeper, Frank Robinson, named the mixture Coca-Cola and wrote it out in his distinctive script.

To this day, Coca-Cola is written the same way. In the first year, Pemberton sold just nine glasses of Coca-Cola a day. A century later, The Coca-Cola Company has produced more than ten billion gallons of syrup. Over the course of three years, between 1888-1891, Atlanta businessman Asa Griggs Candler secured rights to the business for a total of about $2,300 (about £1,500). Candler would become Coca-Cola's first president and the first to bring real vision to the business and the brand.

BUSINESS PORTFOLIO

Take photos of every event you organise from all different angles, outside, inside, front, back, sideways on etc... Then pick out the best pictures and make a portfolio, as this is a great closer for when you do your site survey. Simply show your potential client your previous successful events where you have provided cover. Try to use a high quality camera so these can eventually be added to your website, or even used on advertisements.

An iPad or tablet make great sales tools for showing clients your work, you can even add some testimonials on the tablet for extra impact of your sales pitch. Credibility is one of the most important things you need to establish in order to attract clients to hire your services or use your product for the first time.

Showcasing your skills and capabilities as a professional and as a company through an impressive and factual business portfolio will help you in building your credibility. Having all the right information present in your portfolio can turn this into a dynamic and effective tool to communicate to your target market what you and your company can do for them.

So what should your portfolio contain? Here is your checklist for your website.

1. Provide an overview of what your company is about. This information is useful when introducing your company to potential clients who may not be familiar with your business. This section should discuss your company's history, its founders, a detailed description of what your company does, the number of employees, locations you serve, and what purpose your business serves on the current market, and any special achievements to date.

2. Your business portfolio should also contain accredited memberships like the Chamber of Commerce background and credentials. Include training courses you have completed,

certifications and awards you have earned.

3. Every company should have a mission statement, objectives, and a list of values and standards that will serve as its guide. This will give your potential customers an idea of what they can expect when doing business with your company, and can build trust

4. The most important part of your business portfolio would be the section for your products and services. It is very important to provide a detailed description of what's on offer so your customer can make an informed decision. If you don't advertise it, they don't see it, its difficult to see if someone is smiling in the dark right?

IMPORTANT REFERRAL BUSINESS

The great news about a successful event is that you end up with a satisfied customer. This should be good news for getting repeat business from your customer. The even better news is that you can use your satisfied customers to find you even more satisfied customers! You can get new customers from cold calling but it is far easier to work from referrals.

Every single customer you have is a source of referrals. You can use your satisfied customers to introduce you to their contacts. Customers who have benefited from your product and service are usually more than happy to refer you to their colleagues, friends and acquaintances. If you look at it from the customer's perspective, why wouldn't they want to recommend you?

When you are a customer and you receive good service or buy a really great product you wouldn't hesitate to make a recommendation to people you know. You would want to do it because you want your family, friends or colleagues to get the same benefits that you did!

So remember these simple rules:

Ask for a referral especially when you have received good feedback.

Every customer is a source for referrals. Your customers are a gold mine of referrals, so it is worth spending some time to master the art of mining that gold.

It is recommended that referral generation should be done or suggested when you have erected the structures, when the customer is feeling particularly good about the decision they have made.

You need to get the customer into the right mind-set to recall people who they can refer you and here are some ways to do just that.

How to get a referral from your customer:

"Hello Mr/Ms/Mrs (name)
You have been in the (industry/business/area) for many years. I guess that you have met lots of other (insert trade/position etc) haven't you? If I asked for details of four or five of these people, is this something you could do?"

Note the use of *If I asked you.* The *If* softens the request. You are not directly asking the customer to write them down, you are merely exploring the possibility.

Or, if you feel confident, you could use a more bold approach below.

You: "Would you happen to know two or three people who might be interested in our service"?

You "Would you have their telephone numbers?"

Once you have the referral details:

"Thanks, is it all right if to use your name so Fred knows to take my call?
Customer: "Yes, that's fine - say hello from me."
It really is that simple, and can have an incredible impact on the growth of your business.

WANTED: A WOMAN'S INTUITION

Does anyone know why there are so few women working in the events industry? As the owner of a marquee business, which supplies the event industry, it never ceases to amaze me how few women the industry attracts.

We have helped to set up dozens of marquee hire businesses across the UK and Europe over the past twenty years. Yet not one of these companies are owned or managed by a woman, except for one lady who recently set a hiring company up in Australia. But there are still no female Gala Tent hirers in the UK. So what's the reason? Perhaps the events industry may be suffering from an image crisis – traditionally it's seen as involving working unsociable hours – including evenings and weekends and being a heavy, dirty job, especially when it comes to erecting and dismantling marquees and gazebos. The reality is actually quite different!

Developments in the manufacture of marquees and gazebos mean they feature innovative designs and can be quickly and easily erected by two or more people – women or men! Also, the flexible working hours and the seasonality of the job also means it can work well for mums fitting around school hours.

Many women have great social networks, which means that they could soon turn hosting children's parties, anniversaries, reunions or small weddings into a great marquee hire business. With only a relatively small investment, they could find this pays for itself in hardly any time at all!

All industries need a balance and the events industry, particularly in the UK, needs to sharpen up its act to attract more women. There are huge opportunities for women who have taken redundancy or a career break after having children, to get back into the workplace by setting up a business hiring out marquees and gazebos for domestic or corporate events. Many people find that although this may start as a hobby, it soon becomes a lucrative career where they can make as much income as they would by working a nine to five job. There is a desperate need to change perceptions and show the many opportunities that lie in this sector.

Women have a natural flair towards the event industry, due to their great organisational and planning skills, as well as having fantastic attention to detail and great customer service skills – all key attributes needed by those working in the event industry. I really think as a sector we need to raise awareness of the opportunities, so women can help what is a great industry to become even better.

In our organisation, we employ around 40% women – working in roles from finance to sales. We also find it difficult to attract more women when we're recruiting as, again women do not seem to be attracted to the events industry.

So what can be done? The events industry certainly needs to publicise more widely the opportunities it has for women and this needs to start earlier – in schools, with industry ambassadors talking to female students in particular about roles in the industry. As a business, Gala Tent has set out a plan to help set up at least twelve UK-based female-owned businesses in the marquee hire industry in the next twelve months – are you up for the challenge?

WINNING LOCAL GOVERNMENT CONTRACTS

The public sector includes bodies ranging from central government departments and the NHS to local authorities, emergency services and the military. Together these sectors spent over £220bn per annum directly on orders with small and medium-sized businesses (10% of Government expenditure per year). The Government has committed to increasing this to 25% of all Government spending. Here's how you can improve your chances of getting a piece of the action:

- Find out about contracts. If you have a specific sector in mind, contact the appropriate public body to see what contracts are available. These are also sometimes advertised in the national, local or trade press, so get into the habit of checking.
- Use an outside agency. Consider using commercial organisations that charge a small fee to search for contracts on your behalf. For more information on how to do this, visit the Business Information Publications website.

- Scan Internet databases for contract opportunities. Search the EU Contracts and Tenders database on the EU website or Tenders Electronic Daily.
- Ask your local council. Check local authority websites, these can be a good source of orders. Many of these organisations have booklets or details online that explain how you can become a supplier.

- Don't be put off by the paperwork. Tendering is not always time-consuming and complex. Sometimes it might just mean providing a quote.

- Blow your own trumpet. Demonstrate clearly that you can fulfil the contract in your tender application. Contracts are awarded on the basis of value for money - which means getting the right balance between price and quality.

- Follow the rules. Provide all the information required by the tender and stick to deadlines. You need to have "white folder" policies in place, which means being able to show you have a good record on such things as equal opportunities and health and safety, and insurance.

- Seek advice. The department for Business, Innovation and Skills has a free guide Tendering for Public Contracts. You could also consult your trade body, or seek support from an specialist agency.

- Be realistic. Don't tender for contracts your business is unable to fulfil.

- Ask for feedback. Ensure you ask for feedback if you're unsuccessful with a tender. Public-sector bodies are obliged to provide you with this information.

PCI-DSS COMPLIANCE

The Payment Card Industry Data Security Standards (PCI DSS) is a set of requirements for protecting payment account data security. These standards were developed by the PCI Security Standards Council, an organisation founded by American Express, Discover Financial Services, JCB International, MasterCard Worldwide, and Visa International, to facilitate industry-wide adoption of consistent data security measures on a global basis.

The Payment Card Industry Data Security Standard (PCI DSS) applies to companies of any size that accept credit card payments. If your company intends to accept card payment, and store, process and transmit cardholder data, you need to host your data securely with a PCI compliant hosting provider. The PCI Data Security Standards help protect the safety of that data. They set the operational and technical requirements for organizations accepting or processing payment transactions, and for software developers and manufacturers of applications and devices used in those transactions. Maintaining payment security is serious business. It is vital that every entity responsible for the security of cardholder data diligently follows the PCI Data Security Standards.

Who needs to be PCI DSS compliant?

PCI DSS compliance is a contractual obligation, generally between a Merchant and their Acquiring Bank. It applies to ALL entities that store, process and or transmit payment card data, irrespective of the quantity of payments processed. PCI DSS also applies to Third Party Service Providers, who support entities that may have outsourced the payment handling process. Outsourcing does not release an entity from their obligation to be certified as compliant. The requirements apply to all acceptance channels, including retail (brick-and-mortar), mail/telephone order (MOTO), and e-commerce.

What happens if I am not compliant?

If you do not comply with the security requirements of the card associations, you put your business and your customers at risk of payment card compromise. Data breaches are becoming more and more frequent, and the reputational damage they can cause to a business can be irreparable. You will also be liable for the cost of the required forensic investigations, fraudulent purchases and the cost of re-issuing cards. You may also lose your card acceptance privileges.

What are the penalties for breaches?

Data breaches are known by varying names. Visa refer to them as Account Data Compromise (ADC), whereas MasterCard call them Operational Reimbursement (OR) and Fraud Reimbursement (FR). Penalties vary by card schemes and by the state of compliance at the point of breach. Visa Europe state that a 3000€ penalty would apply for each ADC, which could be followed by a PFI (PCI Forensic Investigation) for Level 1-3 merchants, or for Level 4 merchants who process more than ten thousand Visa cards. Each card then deemed at risk (PAN and CVV2 details) then carries a penalty of 18€.

Example: 30,000 card details breached.
Case Fee: 3000€
ADC Penalties: 30,000 x 18€ = 540,000€

There are hidden costs associated with an ADC event too, including the cost of a full compliance report by engaging a QSA (Qualified Security Assessor) that meets specific information security education requirements, and has taken the appropriate training from the PCI Security Standards

Council, as well as the further migration and development costs to outsourced solutions.

What does 'Descoping' mean?

The PCI DSS considers any person, employee, technology or system that comes into contact with sensitive card data as 'in-scope'. To reduce the amount of applicable PCI controls that must be implemented, businesses are advised by the PCI SSC to reduce whom and what comes into contact with cardholder data.

What is GDPR?

- On May 25th, 2018 the new GDPR (General Data Protection Regulation) became law. Compliance with GDPR is a legal requirement for your business and suppliers.

- Failure to comply could result in huge fines and potential legal action from customers.

- The General Data Protection Regulation is a regulation by which the European Union (EU) intends to strengthen data protection for individuals within the (EU).

- The primary objectives of the GDPR are to give citizens back the control of their personal data and to simplify the regulatory environment for international business.
- It also addresses export of personal data outside the EU – so companies that use offices elsewhere in the world to deal with EU citizens must comply.
- If a company trades in Europe – it must comply, regardless of Brexit

There are two tiers of fines:

Tier 1: up to 2% of annual worldwide turnover or €10,000,000 (whichever is the higher);
Tier 2: up to 4% of annual worldwide turnover or €20,000,000 (whichever is the higher)

In addition to the administrative fines above, GDPR also gives any person who has suffered material or non-material damage as a result of an infringement of the GDPR the right to receive compensation. There is no ceiling on the level of compensation - so the cost to a business could be extremely high.

Regulators have a range of other enforcement powers (e.g. audit rights, order compliance, impose ban on processing)

A data breach is defined as follows:
"...a breach of security leading to the accidental or unlawful destruction, loss, alteration, unauthorised disclosure of, or access to, personal data transmitted, stored or otherwise processed"
If a data breach occurs, the company only has 72 hours from becoming aware of the breach to report it to the regulatory body (In the UK this is the Information Commissioners Office (ICO)). If it is not reported within 72 hours the regulatory body will want to know why.

Taking payments

People don't understand how cancellations effects business and they don't really care. Lots of sole traders suffer from this. Personal trainers are another, therefore gym owners take monthly or annual payments, pay as you go in this sector and the event industry does not work, and you cannot afford a cancellation as a small enterprise and certainly not sole trader.

Here is my suggestion for payment terms.

FIRST PAYMENT - £50 deposit is required to SAVE THE DATE of your client's event. This is very important if someone has a special date for an event. You must offer them the option to book the date there and then after the site survey, or over the phone if circumstances require this. There are only fifty two weekends in a year and only eighteen to twenty in the summer months and these are very valuable to you. And if someone else calls you the next day and wants to book that very same day you cannot afford to turn it away. Oh, and this WILL happen, I can assure you; it happens all the time at Gala Tent with stock. A client will call up for a certain marquee size, frame or maybe particular colour and we will ask them for the sale, and they will say I want to think about it and call back later only to be disappointed that the item is now showing out of stock.

SECOND PAYMENT - 30% deposit required fourteen days after saving the date for any other service agreed. (the £50 only secures the date for fourteen days)

THIRD PAYMENT (c) Remittance of full payment is required six weeks before the event date or before.

Using this method will flush out any time wasters and you will save yourself a lot of grief later down the line as this payment model will prevent any cancellations which will cost you dearly. Six weeks cleared payment can be enough time to book another event, and you have some cash in the bank to cover your costs as despots are non-refundable. If the event falls in the six weeks from the booking date, then just ask for full payment and say "This is quite unusual and I usually have more time to plan but let's skip the save the date, and deposit and get you fully booked now!"

What payment system should I use?

As everything these days is turning digital, I recommend a digital payment system; you don't have the time or want to go to the expense of visiting your client to collect cash. We recommend SOTpay, which you can find here: www.sotpay.co.uk

SOTpay is the only system that can assist
email, text, social media, chat and telephone
payments meeting all PCI DSS Compliance
regulations. I would not recommend PayPal
as your first choice as they charge 3.4% + 20p
for every transaction, and this is huge chuck
of change from your bottom line. However, if
you have a bad credit rating and your
application for a merchant number is refused
from your bank manager then PayPal is the
next best option.

Protect your business at all costs

Taking a SOTpay digital payment will also
protect you from fraud and bogus bookings as
the system verifies the ID of the client even
when they are not present. The other added
benefit is protection from any scheming
jealous enemy or competitor in your area.
You will also have the flexibility to take a
payment on the go as there is a mobile app
that will allow you to make sales on the job.

SOTpay can also be set to accept a card on file,
which means you can securely store your
client's payment details for when they book
again. Don't feel embarrassed for asking for a
payment in advance. Just set your terms
clearly and if you are questioned, you're
within your rights to simply say you like to
get the payment terms out of the way first, so
that you can perform the job without having

to take up any more valuable time later. I even add to this by saying no one likes asking for payment or taking a payment (or worse, chasing a payment) so let's just get that stuff off the table so we can do business together and concentrate on building our relationship.

This is a very true and honest approach and a powerful statement you can't argue with and one everyone can relate to. I will give you another example. I own a few bars and restaurants, gyms and commercial units, which I rent out. I say to all my tenants that I don't like doing any accounting work, and I especially don't like chasing payment as this will damage our relationship in the future. Before any lease is signed, I ask for the lease payments to the paid on the 28th day of each month on a standing order so we don't have to talk about payments ever again, and I add this to the terms of business. This way I only have to login to the bank once a month to tick off all the payments. I personally manage the accounts and it is very easy and I have great relationship with all my tenants as a made sure I future proofed this at the earliest stage.

If you do become a member of the Gala Tent hire network, I will provide you with a full payment terms agreement to offer your client.

TIPS FOR EFFECTIVE RECRUITMENT

Once your business has grown to a certain extent, you will need to start thinking about taking on your first employee. Below is a step-by-step guide to employing somebody for the first time. From how to write a job description to where to hold your interview, here is everything you need to know.

Step one: Write your job role description

There are several ways to advertise employment, such as in a local newspaper, online job sites, email and social media. When advertising for a job you need to make sure that the job description is easy to read and attracts your ideal candidates. Below are some examples of how to write your job description:

- Give a brief summary of all the roles and responsibilities you will expect your employee to carry out.

- Include the hours per day/ week.

- Don't forget to write how to apply for the job – by email or phone? By CV and covering letter or by application form?

- Include the holiday entitlement.

- Where the company is based and where they will have to travel.

- Include the key skills that are needed for the job role.

- Include the good points about the job but also a few bad points such as if it was for a customer service role you could include that the customers are sometimes difficult so you are needing someone who is capable of handling different customers.

Step two: Where to advertise your role

There are multiple websites for job advertisements such as Jobsite, Reed, Totaljobs, or Indeed. Facebook and LinkedIn have become big players in the job advertisement game. Or simply with the Job Centre via the government website. It is best to get your advert on local sites that people see on a day-to-day basis to make your job role more relevant to people in your area.

A great way to advertise a job would be in the local newspaper, this is a great way to expand your audience as more experienced and older people read this on a daily basis and seek more information than what would be put online.

Step three: How to conduct your interview

Once you have a number of candidates that have applied for your job, you can choose and invite the prospective employees in. When you have a number of people coming for interviews on set dates make sure you have planned them out leaving you enough time to reflect upon their responses to your questions, and to refresh your mind to focus on the next candidate.

Ensure that you interview the candidate in a quiet room so that there are no distractions and it is less nerve wracking for the interviewee. Interviewing whilst in a quiet room is a great way to get to know the candidate more and hear more about their achievements and personality to be able to decide whether or not they are right for that job role.

INTERVIEW QUESTIONS

You may be the most confident and successful self-employed businessperson out there when working on your own. You may have once attended a job interview yourself, but the process of interviewing for the ideal candidates to help take your business to the next level can often be an arduous and intimidating process. You are now looking to bring people into the fold who buy into, and value your vision for the future of the business, so the information you get from them is important.

Think about the kind of people you would like to surround yourself with when working. Do you want somebody who is best working off his or her own steam or somebody who's happiest working with others? Would you want somebody who will follow your instructions to the letter or would you prefer them to take ownership of tasks? The interview is one of the most important processes in taking your business to that next level, as the workforce you bring in will be entrusted with responsibilities that you've been used to taking on alone, but eventually you will need to do it, if you want your business to evolve from successful lone trader to successful multi-million pound operation.

Here are some helpful pieces of information and questions that could assist with securing you the best workforce. Remember, we can all be good at an interview if we think we know what an interviewer wants to hear, so push for a candidate to elaborate further on their as much as you can.

Helpful pre-interview information

Name: **Date:**   **Time:**

**Candidate
Name:**

**Candidate
Title:**   **Phone Number:**

**Position Applied
For:**

**Required
Skills:**

Suggested Questions

Question: Tell me about yourself?

This is an obvious one to start with. It's an open request that gives your candidate the opportunity to speak about a familiar subject, which is themselves. Listen to how your interviewee speaks about their life and how much they are willing to divulge.

Question: What do you know about/Why would you like to join this company?

This is a very important question to know how your candidate has prepared for the interview, and therefore how they might approach any future opportunity when they work for you. Any prospective employee should spend their own time prior to the interview researching your company, showing a willingness to learn. An effective interviewee will know your organisation inside and out, which gives a great idea of how they might follow up on leads and other opportunities to bring business to you. There's nothing worse than an open-mouthed blank look from a candidate who thinks they only have to show up to get the job!

Question: What can you contribute to this company?

The candidate should get the opportunity to sing their own praises in their own words. You will likely have a list of ideal qualities either written down or mentally stored, so be sure to check them off and dig further if they come up.

Question: What do you think are your weaknesses?

Another classic interview question; we can all talk about how great we are, but it's a lot tougher to think about what we are not so good at. Don't be suckered in by responses such as *I'm too much of a perfectionist* or something which creates a negative from too much positive. You want your candidate to be honest, so push for them to elaborate on their responses.

Question: Give some examples of when you went over and above to… (insert ideal quality here)?

This forces the candidate to think about past success, and their part in achieving it. Push them with digging follow up questions such as *and how did that make you feel?* This is an invaluable part of getting a candidate to open up beyond practised responses to what they think you might ask.

Question: Why did you leave your last job?

A good response to this question will give you an insight into the kind of potential employee you have before you, and their prospects for remaining a part of your operation for years to come. People leave roles for many reasons, such as greater pay, less restrictive hours, redundancy or proximity to their home. They also leave because they were terrible employees and were no longer suited to their role. Listen carefully to their response and take the information on board.

SPREADING THE COST

My company Gala Tent Ltd can provide individually tailored finance packages that can massively help with your business start-up. These finance packages range for interest free twelve month options through to interest bearing five year Buy Now Pay Later options, so there's always likely to be an option that suits your business plan.

You only have to pay a small deposit with a finance agreement; this enables you to choose the best equipment available with only a small initial cash outlay. You are then able to have the best equipment available with the latest technology and start to enjoy the extra profits this generates before your next payment is due.

How does it work?

Find the products that you would like to purchase and add them to your shopping basket. If the basket total is as little as £350, you can consider the option of using Duologi to purchase your goods. You don't even have to do this during business hours! Our finance application system can be completed at any time, through the Gala Tent website.

If you are approved for finance you will need to have your payment card ready to leave a deposit (minimum of 10%). You can then pay the remainder as monthly payments, with a loan duration of your choice.

How much does it cost?

It depends on the scheme that you select when making the credit application. The monthly costs will be clearly shown to you in the application process so that you can decide on the scheme that best suits your needs.

Full finance details, including actual monthly repayments and total cost are shown within the application process.

What if I have a bad credit score?

It is less likely that you will be approved for finance if your credit score is lower than Fair, but rejection is no guarantee. The Duologi application process will check your credit record at the point that you submit your application. If your credit score is poor your application may be referred to an underwriter or even declined. If you feel this was in error then we recommend contacting Citizens Advice who will be able to help you understand your credit history and correct any errors.

Can anybody apply?

To apply for finance you must meet the following criteria:
You must be over eighteen years of age. You must be a UK resident with at least three years continual address history. You must be in full time employment, unless retired or a house person with a spouse in full time employment.
You must have a UK bank account capable of accepting Direct Debits. The goods must be delivered to your home address.

Choose the finance that suits you

Using our simple Duologi calculator, you can choose from a minimum of 10% deposit through to a maximum of 50%. You can also determine the finance period. As you make your selections the calculator will display all the relevant repayment details.

Will this application leave a footprint on my credit record?

Yes, as with many credit searches, your credit record will be affected whatever the result, so it is important that you are optimistic of passing the credit check, to reduce the potential for your credit rating being adversely affected by a rejection.

What happens if my credit application is rejected?

You will be able to return to checkout and use a credit or debit card, or PayPal to complete your transaction, and continue on your road to business success!

Is a deposit required?

Yes. A minimum 10% deposit is payable by credit or debit card upon acceptance.

How are my monthly payments made?

All monthly payments are paid by direct debit from your personal bank account. Typically the first payment will be due one month after the date of the finance agreement and subsequent monthly payments will be due every month for the length of your term on that day of the month.

What type of equipment can I purchase?

Pretty much everything you need to start up your hiring business; marquees, gazebos, equipment and accessories. Any customised product, such as flags, banners, or printed gazebo canopies, must be purchased up front. Acceptance for purchasing goods on finance is subject to status and provided by the finance company.

SECTION TWO:

Case Studies

GARY STRANGEMAN

BOUNCEROO

Q. How did you start the company and how much did you invest?

A. It's difficult to know where to start really, but basically I was looking for a new challenge.

In that year, my mother in law was seventy, so we decided to have a party for her in the back garden and as a result we purchased a Gala Tent marquee. Everyone had a great time. During the party, one person came up and said that the marquee was great and I should consider hiring it out. I later spoke to the wife who said that I was mad but I did some research and found that there were lots of companies doing the large traditional marquees, but very few for the small garden party type events. So I decided to start a small business hiring children's bouncy castles and small marquees. I did some local advertising and because I knew the different sizes of marquees I could get from Gala Tent, if I had an enquiry for a particular size I would buy one and do the job, and that is how I built up my stock of marquees to the point where I can now offer fifteen different sizes and I have on hire five of the most popular sizes at any given time.

To set up the business cost £6,199.39 but that did include over £3000 for the bouncy castles, and as the enquiries came in I purchased the necessary equipment to do it. I have tried to add an additional service each year and we are now able to offer not only bouncy castles and marquees but banqueting hire, mobile bars, discos, hot and cold catering, dance floors and two members of my family have trained and become wedding balloon decorators. I have found that over the last couple of years we are being asked to do more and more weddings so we now offer wedding linings.

Q. Why would an organiser choose Gala Tent?

A. I think price nowadays is very important and the fact that we now offer just about everything a customer would want in one place, a one stop shop if you like. I know other companies do a similar thing but most supply one element themselves and sub contract the rest where as we actually provide all the services ourselves so we keep control of our high standards.

Q. What are your plans for the future?

A. I would like to buy a large frame tent for the bigger weddings rather than having to put together more than one marquee to achieve the same size four large 6m x 12m marquees with three slightly smaller ones for catering is our record to beat. I think we are going to match that this year with a wedding in Kent. I would also like to build the corporate customer side of the business because although we have done work for the likes of the local councils and NHS most of our present work comes from the private sector.

Q. Do you have any events logistical issues?

A. There have been so many events of all different kinds each normally comes with its own set of problems whether it be timings or available space. One of the most challenging was one that was a corporate party for local business in Norwich. They required three 4m x 6m marquees erected on a flat roof situated at least three stories up. There was no access for us through the building with the equipment, therefore we had to set up scaffolding with ladders at the rear of the premises and manhandled every pole up to the roof and obviously back down again. We received the below testimonial from the organiser.

" I asked Bounceroo to provide marquee covering on a roof terrace for a party, where space and weight restrictions applied. Service was exceptional, from the site visit to discussing requirements, to the erection and dismantling of the equipment. Bounceroo were very professional, helpful and friendly and we will definitely use them again and would not hesitate in recommending them."

Q. How do you see the event industry in a few years from now?

A. I think the event industry will be fine. Of course, an increased price doesn't help any business and people will have tighter budgets, but I think overall the event industry will be here for a long time to come.

JUSTIN HARRIS

GARDEN PARTY HIRE

Q. How did you get started in the Event Industry?

A. One of my earliest childhood memories was of one of my birthdays and my mother arranging a party at home for me. I didn't join in the games, why would I? It was my party for the enjoyment of my friends. Not so strange then that I end up years later with my own event company providing parties for the enjoyment of others.

Having finally moved home into our first very modest semi from a top floor flat, to finally have our very own garden was bliss. The builders had eventually returned the keys after a lengthy renovation; this signalled the start of the planning for our very first house party in the garden as I had just fitted brand new carpets in the house.

I started to buy tables, chairs & a couple of small marquees from Gala Tent, all suitable for a party at home, a garden party. A close friend of senior years called in for a cuppa and I showed him with pride the tables &

chairs stacked waiting for the party, "fantastic idea, rent them out"! A friendly but slightly heated discussion ensued; I was convinced I'd won. After all, it was for my party, no-one else's.

A couple of weeks later I received a call from my friendly local pub landlord. It seemed a barmaid was emigrating to New Zealand with her husband to start a new life and wanted a decent send off in the pub garden. An invite perhaps? After all I was a regular in the pub, but no, the landlord had offered to hire the young lady my marquees, tables & chairs!!

I was adamant that this was not happening, protesting with polite force. Every man has his price, apparently mine is £300 and it was a done deal before I answered my phone. Later I discovered the lady in question had invited over a hundred guests, the ladies to be wearing ball gowns and the gent's black ties and I owned just one 6m x 4m and one 6m x 3m Gala Tent Marquee complete with guttering kit! How on earth were we going to fit over a hundred people and a disco into the marquees?

I am quite well known for being true to my word and I'm equally well known for not doing things by half. Couldn't let the young lady down, could we? So I then set out and bought three 6m x 12m Gala Tent Marquees plus an entrance marquee, two dance floors, banqueting tables, additional chairs, flooring, chandeliers and rope lights.

My home was now filled with Gala Tents and equipment. Our reward for this lunacy was indeed £300 plus a welcome bonus of £100, a case of beer & a bouquet of flowers for my wife. Totally unnecessary, but most appreciated none the less.

For the next few years our phone rang quite regularly with requests for the loan of marquee equipment. If we couldn't fulfil the requests I just bought the necessary kit so as not to let anyone down. Eventually, when our garage was full, and likewise the dining room, spare room and the lounge was looking pretty full too, we had a decision to make. We'd met some very nice people along the way, and the work was enjoyable and rewarding so we decided to "go for it" with nothing to lose other than money of course. We rented a council owned warehouse and moved in. We filled one square corner, and then panicked with the realisation of just what we'd done. What had we done?

However, in for a penny, so we invested a few thousand pounds more, "live life on the edge," they say, as the views are fantastic. The only trouble is, I'm scared of heights! Oh well, minor problem, close your eyes and hold on tight, it's bound to get a little bumpy along the way!

The banks are not very supportive towards a new start up business, one famous piece of bankers' advice to help cash flow was to sell off equipment in winter and then replace it the next year, fortunately we didn't take up that piece of advice.

We have always delivered on time and in good order. Even when, one year, I was very ill but upon recovery I was straight back into the office to check deliveries for one of our busiest times - Christmas Eve, I was adamant we would not let anyone down.

Now, ten years on from our first event, we have over £400,000 worth of stock and increasing, and we're in need of larger premises. We can count numerous blue chip companies as very regular clients across the country; we've even worked for, and fed, "A-list" Celebrities including Marco Pierre White and Liz Hurley, each to their complete satisfaction.

From helping people with small Garden Parties to organising complete events for blue chip companies for five thousand people, Garden Party Hire is a real and very profitable business created by friends persuading me into helping others.

The honesty and integrity of our approach has led to repeat business, even during the recession. Many of our clients give us the brief outline of their events and leave the rest to us, including the budget. We don't spend thousands on advertising; we've never made a single sales call in our lives. We used to have a conversion rate from enquiry to booking of 89%, this has now risen to 93% and we currently average two hundred and fifty marquee hire jobs per year with an average transaction value of £700.

We now employ chefs and this year we have plans to get our chefs working harder; our new menus are due to be launched in the next couple of months. They will include buffets, BBQ's and sit-down meals for both private clients and corporate. You won't find anything obvious or boring, but you will find good honest simple tasty food, all cooked from quality fresh ingredients. We don't employ cooks; only qualified, quality chefs. Good old-fashioned customer service, some say it's back in fashion – we say it never went out!

Plans for future include expansion of the marquee hire business, which will require more investment in Gala Tents and equipment, and we have further expansion plans for the catering side of the business.

The event industry, particularly in our specialised field, was never affected by the recent recessions or Brexit, and I don't see a downturn in the foreseeable future.

DAVID BLACKETT

SAWTRY MARQUEES LTD

Q. Why did you start a marquee hire company?

A. I had enough of working for bosses that abused their position. It just so happened that I, and two friends, had bought two small marquees to use for our own personal parties; we set up a small part time hire business in the village to help pay for the marquees. It was seeing this venture, albeit small, work well that I decided to start my own Marquee Hire business. My friends helped me get it off the ground but had other ventures they were pursuing.

Q. How much did you invest?

A. Initially my investment was small. I already had two marquees and I bought items as I needed them by reinvesting. I operated out of my garage and bought a trailer for £500. I would say that over the last seven years I have invested just over £20,000.

Q. Why did you choose Gala Tent?

A. My first two marquees were not from Gala

Tent, I only found them later (in my journey). I switched to Gala Tent because of the quality of the PVC and range of sizes they stocked. I have recently invested in the even stronger Fusion Marquees. For me the pricing helps to ensure that I can afford to build a business with a quick return on investment.

Q. What was your turn over while working part time?

A. I was turning over around £30,000 to £35,000 working weekends, which really surprised me as I was earning more than I was in my full time employment role.

Q. What was your marketing plan?

A. Simple, there are loads of marquee companies in my area offering fantastic marquee hire, but no one catering for the smaller garden market. I have continued down this route but have now expanded by introducing the Fusion Marquee to allow me to pick up work for the larger weddings, corporate and hospitality business.

Q. What works which you have found most effective?

A. What seems to work for me is to keep it simple and provide a more personal approach, go that extra mile for the customer to earn that repeat business or referral.

Q. Do you have any logistical issues?

A. There will always be logistical issues the bigger your marquee hire business gets. The main one being storage, and have I got enough vans and manpower to help through the year. I face these issues each year as the business grows, however each year we work through them.

Q. Did your business suffer through the recession?

A. Hard to say because I have been going for only seven years and the first three years I was only working part time; so when I really threw myself in to it, we were already in a recession. I may not have loads of money piled up in banks but each year I increase my sales and make a good profit.

Q. What prompted you to go in to the Marquee Hire business full time?

A. I arranged a meeting with Jason Mace which helped me to see a clearer picture of what I intend to achieve for my marquees hire company. I placed an order to expand my range there and then and never looked back.

Q. What are your views on how the event industry will hold up?

A. I believe that marquees will always offer customers with an alternative to celebrate at home; if we stop talking ourselves into a recession all the time more people will spend just that little bit more on the event rather than holding back.

MARTIN NICHOLLS

PARTY ON MARQUEE HIRE

Q. Why did you start a marquee hire company?

A. Seemed like a good idea at the time and this was something we felt we could do.

Q. How much did you invest?

A. Our initial investment was £2,000 in the first year, £10,000 for each subsequent year.

Q. Why did you choose Gala Tent?

A. I was unaware there was anyone else that had that quality and product range.

Q. What was your marketing plan?

A. Internet, yellow pages advertising aiming at garden parties and small budget weddings, I have since moved on to more corporate events.

Q. What works which you have found most effective?

A. Internet advertising (Google, marquee hire

portals) and being nice to people, wins repeat business.

Q. What plans for next year?

A. Expansion with higher range of traditional and stylish bespoke structures, we have 75m x 6m of Gala Tent so its time to add more variety.

Q. Do you have any logistical issues?

A. None that we can't solve.

Q. Has your business been effected by the recession?

A. Well we've grown by around 20% per year on average over the last 5 years so I would have to say no - however you have to keep your prices competitive despite costs going up.

Q. What is your turnover for close of business in your first year?

A. Turnover was £77,000 and close of business the following year was £120,000.

Q. What are your views on how the event industry will hold up this year?

A. Our bookings are around 20% up on last year to date - so I think we should be ok.

People are being more realistic about their weddings and rather than booking expensive hotels meaning more business for where we are pitched in the market place.

MARK HAMMOND

ABACUS PARTY COVER

Q. What was your turnover in your first year of trading?

A. Turnover in the 1st year working part time was - £11,413.44

Q. What was your turnover in the second year?

A. Turnover in the 2nd year was £32,000

Q. Why did you start a marquee hire company?

A. After looking at venues such as town halls, sport clubs etc for holding a birthday party, I quickly realised that as well as the expense in the hiring out of the venue, there are regulations that hinder many events (such as out-by-midnight, not allowing U18's etc). Holding an event in your home seemed the only option as it gave so much more flexibility and after a bit of research into small marquee hire there seemed to be a niche market where I live (Hertfordshire).

Q. How much did you invest?

A. Initially it was from personal savings from a part time job of around £1200. After A-Levels the age of 18 with no other savings and absolutely no chance of a bank loan of even £2,500, for the first year the business was on the basis of make some money, invest it into more marquees, make some more money, spend some more etc. Investment into equipment to date is approximately £8500.

Q. Why did you choose Gala Tent?

A. Several reasons. Other manufacturers provide many similar marquees in terms of appearance, (although about 10% more expensive). But in regards to design they were lacking in comparison. One example would be the side panels, they bungee the side of the panels to the 'C' pole, Gala Tent have a zip or Dutch lacing ensuring no draught can get through which is one of the main reason my Gala Tents are brilliant in the winter. I've just had a customer complain last month it was too hot for her (what can I do?). Also, one of the biggest USP that Gala Tent should be proud of is ability to order spare parts. Being in the hire industry I am forever in need of spares parts due to wear and tear or malicious damage. This is something I'm eternally grateful for, as other suppliers would only sell the whole marquee, which obviously isn't cost effective if you're only requiring one or two parts. Also, I like how all Gala Tent marquees are always in stock, I can order it on Monday for next day delivery and I know it will be here.

Q. What was your marketing plan?

A. I'm quite lucky that at this moment in time, in terms of the small marquee hire market I enjoy little competition. So I do not have to spend lots of hard earned cash on expensive Google campaigns. I'm forever being told by customers that as soon as they had seen my website I was exactly what they were looking for. So getting myself known was a priority and by having a good online prominence was and still is a major marketing strategy for me. This consists on enhanced SEO work, Google Adwords, marquee hire comparison sites and other advertising media such as Yellow Pages/Yell.com and various magazine advertisements. I think half the time hiring a marquee in your own home isn't even an option for some people as they assume the word 'marquee' means large and expensive such as a typical wedding marquee. By trying to put the message across that you can have a marquee in your own home from around £150 is what I am still aiming to do.

Q. What works which you have found most effective?

A. Google is by far the most effective way in getting in traffic to the website and getting me enquiries. It's when people find me and realise what we are here for – to extend your home instantly is the reason why we get quite a number of enquires. My marquee comparison website I am involved in gives me a lot of leads on a daily basis as well as yell.com getting me lots of hits particularly now as it's been designed for today's market – searching via mobile devices (iPhones, iPads & other smart phones etc).

Q. What are plans for next year?

A. Our plans are to continue adding to my vast list of extras we have to offer in the marquee. I'm currently planning on LED Cube Seating, artificial plants and I am also looking to extend my range of business services I offer through local companies I have 'under my wing'. I want to create that 'one stop shop' service whatever the event may be, so by doing the above shall help me create this service. Also I aim to give more of a choice in terms of marquee range. Whether that would mean increasing the amount of sizes I have, or I'm also very keen into investing into Gala Tent's Fusion Marquees. By doing this I think I shall be ready to confidently approach the wedding marquee market, more towards the 'moderately priced weddings', as I have already found a location where we can regularly use it for wedding/marquee hire.

Q. Do you have any logistical issues?

A. Oh yes! Given the fact I'm only 20 years old hinders what I can potentially carry to a job. This is because of my age being so young I am restricted into what type of vehicle I can drive. I currently use a Peugeot Expert van which for the time being is fine but as the business grows, the size of the marquees may increase as well as the amount of products I offer to put inside them will too. In turn I need a larger van to carry the increased amount but I simply cannot find anyone to insure me to drive a larger van presently. This is currently the only thing hindering me buying more products to offer as running to a job 2-3 times isn't cost or time effective at all. Hopefully in when I'm 21 may help this issue.

Q. Has your business been effected by the recession?

A. I started the business in the middle of the recession! By looking at my first year's turnover in comparison to my projected turnover - is showing a steep growth already. I have every confidence in Abacus Party Cover to keep on growing even in these hard times. Having an event such as a party is a luxury to anyone, and this type of expense would always be the first to go from anybody's budget if things get tougher, so I always have to bear that in mind but by introducing discounts and special offers particularly in out of season times of the year helps to keep the business an on-going success. The increasing fuel prices as well as all other business expenses which are constantly rising doesn't help things at all so it is always in the back of my mind whether next year will be harder.

Q. What are your views on how the event industry will hold up in the next few years?

A. Well everybody gets married; everybody has parties - they will never vanish so I have every confidence that the event industry will still be a successful sector. Speaking from personal experience during my second year in business I am already getting repeat business as well as business spread from word of mouth. This I believe should increase year on year as more people are impressed by our service and recommend to others. I always try to give the best possible customer service as word of mouth advertising may have a huge impact in what the future has for Abacus Party Cover.

May I take this opportunity to thank Jason and Gala Tent in helping me start my small marquee hire business and I look forward to many more successful years between us.

KEITH WILSON AND GARY MITCHELL

WEALD EVENT HIRE

Gala Tent helped business partners Keith Wilson and Gary Mitchell set up their own marquee hire company, Weald Event Hire. The pair started laying the foundations of their business with a visit to Gala Tent HQ in February, which culminated in the purchase of two 6mx18m marquees and a host of accessories.

Weald Event Hire is a Marquees and Catering venture which offers services suitable for Birthdays, Anniversaries, Garden and Dinner Parties, Communal, Charitable and Corporate Events in and around Uckfield, East Sussex and covering the towns and villages of nearby Kent and West Sussex.

Keith gave us an insight into Weald Event Hirer's operation:
"It's been a really exciting time for me and Gary, we've been really busy carrying out an extensive local marketing campaign of both digital and conventional media, leafleting and personal contacts. As with any new start-up it can take time to build a customer base and

reputation but we're happy with our progress thus far and we're already taking bookings, which is fantastic!"

Having already owned and managed a string of successful businesses in his own right, Keith teamed up with co-owner Gary Mitchell on this new joint venture.

Gary told us more about his past experiences: "I've spent a lifetime in the hospitality industry, the last twenty of which has been in my home town, managing a local function suite and restaurants for other people. I thought that it was time for a bit of a shake up and that's where Gala Tent came in, marquees as a venue seemed flexible, affordable and increasingly popular, it was an ideal choice." "It has been really exciting for myself and Keith so far and I'm optimistic about the future, things are really starting to come together nicely."

Q. Why did you choose Gala Tent?

A: From Gary's extensive experience and my more recent personal one, marquees as a venue seemed flexible, affordable and increasingly popular. We chose Gala on price, flexibility and service.

Q. What was the motivation to start your own business?

A. We started planning the business with my first visit to Gala in February and had our first booking on Saturday the 11th of June. We knew each other and had discussed other alternatives, as Gary eventually wanted to have his own business and I'd had businesses before, it seemed like the perfect lifestyle business after finding myself bored in retirement.

TIM DRAYCOTT

SHROPSHIRE HOG ROASTS

Shropshire Hog Roasts, the garden marquee hire and outdoor catering company, has reported a significant increase in business this year, with the company already fully booked for the next six months.

Tim Draycott spent twenty years catering for major events before he started his own business eight years ago with his partner Amanda. He has invested in a number of Gala Tent marquees over the years, because he liked the product and the price and now owns fourteen in different sizes. Tim Draycott said: "Our aim is to provide a first class events and catering service, whilst keeping it affordable. I know I've achieved this because we're so busy, with so many repeat booking and personal recommendations coming through all the time."

At a time when some marquee companies charge for every single item, Shropshire Hog Roast prides itself on offering a complete package with no hidden extras. Tim said: "We provide everything from catering, tables, chairs, marquee decorations, lighting, bunting, flooring, snow machines.... you name it, we've usually got it! It's what makes our marquees and hog Roasts so popular."

Shropshire Hog Roasts finds that at least sixty per cent of their business comes from referrals. Tim adds: "Some people insist on having us for their weddings and parties, they'd rather change the date than go with anyone else. It's really flattering that they think of our services so highly!"

Before he got into catering, Tim worked for a couple of years as a scaffolder, so is used to carrying around a lot of poles and equipment around. He says: "I can erect a 6m x 10m marquee in just 16 minutes. I find the marquees durable, easy to erect and most importantly to my business, they are safe and fully water protected. I get so many fantastic comments from my clients about how they like the quality of them. What makes it so rewarding for me is seeing the smiles on people's faces when their event has been a massive success."

Jason Mace, Managing Director of Gala Tent, said: "It is fantastic to hear how well that Shropshire Hog Roasts is doing. Tim has a great business model, combining his expertise in catering with marquee and event hire. Our products are affordable so that companies like Shropshire Hog Roasts can benefit from durable marquees that are popular with customers, but which mean they can keep their prices competitive. We wish Tim and Amanda all the best for the future."

Tim's marquees are booked out every week, apart from his quieter months, which are usually January and February, when he concentrates on supplying nightclub decor and also snow and bubble machines to clubs around the area.

Tim adds: "Garden marquee parties are becoming more popular, as people like the fact that they're less formal and also that they don't cost as much as hiring a venue. In the past, we've done a lot of festivals, but now we are focusing more on weddings, anniversaries, street parties and live music events. We've hosted some really top name bands in our marquees the past few weeks, including the Arctic Monkeys, and it's just fantastic to see people having such a good time at an event we have created for them." Tim continues: "I'd like to franchise our business model one day, as we have a proven recipe for success and it would really take the business to the next level and on a national basis."

There are many advantages of being a Gala Tent trade customer, which includes receiving priority sales leads, automatic discount off every purchase, exclusive offers throughout the year that are available to members only and ongoing support with marketing.

SECTION THREE:

The Legal Stuff

CHOOSING A LEGAL STRUCTURE FOR YOUR NEW BUSINESS

You must choose a business structure when you start a business. The structure you choose will define your legal responsibilities, such as:

- The paperwork you must fill in to get started
- The taxes you'll have to manage and pay
- How you can personally take the profit your business makes
- Your personal responsibilities if your business makes a loss

Types of business

Most businesses in the UK are:

- Sole traders
- Limited companies
- Business partnerships

> - If you're setting up a small
>   organisation like a sports club or a
>   voluntary group and don't plan to
>   make a profit, you can form an
>   'unincorporated association'.

What counts as self-employed?

You are self-employed if you:

> - Run your business for yourself and
>   take responsibility for its success or
>   failure
> - Have several customers at the same
>   time
> - Can decide how, where and when you
>   do your work
> - Can hire other people to do the work
>   for you or help you at your own
>   expense
> - Provide the main items of equipment
>   to do your work
> - Are responsible for finishing any
>   unsatisfactory work in your own time
> - Charge an agreed fixed price for your
>   work
> - Sell goods or services to make a profit.

You can be both employed and self-employed at the same time, for example if you work for an employer during the day and run your own business in the evenings.

Selling goods or services

You could be classified as a trader if you're selling goods or services regularly, e.g.:

- Online
- At car boot sales
- Through classified adverts

If you're trading, you're self-employed.

What counts as trading

You're likely to be trading if you:

- Sell regularly to make a profit
- Make items to sell for profit
- Earn commission from selling goods for other people
- Are paid for a service you provide

You're probably not trading if you sell some unwanted items occasionally.

What you need to do

To register as self-employed, you'll need to:

> - Tell HMRC to make sure you pay the correct Income Tax and National Insurance through Self Assessment
> - Keep records of your business income and outgoings
> - Pay your tax each year, usually in 2 payments on the 31 January and 31 July - use HMRC's calculator to help you budget for this

VAT

You must register for VAT if your business turnover is over £81,000. You can register voluntarily if it suits your business, e.g. you sell to other VAT-registered businesses and want to reclaim the VAT.

What is a limited company?

A limited company is an organisation that you can set up to run your business.
It's responsible in its own right for everything it does and its finances are separate to your personal finances.
The company owns any profit it makes, after it pays Corporation Tax. The company can then share its profits.

Ownership

Every limited company has 'members' - people or organisations who own shares in the company.
Directors are responsible for running the company. Directors often own shares, but they don't have to.

'Ordinary' business partnership

In a business partnership, you and your business partner (or partners) personally share responsibility for your business.
You can share all your business' profits between the partners. Each partner pays tax on his or her share of the profits.
Partnerships in Scotland (known as 'firms') are different, and have a 'legal personality' separate from the individual partners.

Legal responsibilities

You're personally responsible for your share of:

- Any losses your business makes
- Bills for things you buy for your business, like stock or equipment

If you don't want to be personally responsible for a business' losses, you can set up a limited partnership or limited liability partnership.

SETTING UP AS A SOLE TRADER

Sole traders must register with HM Revenue and Customs (HMRC) and follow certain rules on running and naming their business.

If you're a sole trader, you're running your own business as an individual. This is known as being 'self-employed'. You can keep all your business' profits after you've paid tax on them.

You can take on staff - 'sole trader' means you're responsible for the business, not that you have to work alone.

Your responsibilities

You're responsible for:

- Your business debts
- Bills for anything you buy for your business, like stock or equipment
- Keeping records of your business' sales and expenses
- Sending a Self Assessment tax return every year

> - Paying Income Tax on the profits your business makes and National Insurance

Naming your business

You can use your own name or trade under a business name. There are rules on using a business name. For example, you can't:

> - Use the terms 'Limited,' 'Ltd', 'Public Limited Company,' 'PLC,' 'Limited Liability Partnership,' 'LLP' or their Welsh equivalents.
> - Use sensitive words or expressions unless you have permission.
> - Suggest a connection with government or local authorities.
> - Use a name that is too similar to a registered trademark or an existing business in the same area or sector.
> - Use a name that is likely to offend.

You must include your own name and business name (if you have one) on any official paperwork, such as invoices and letters.

SETTING UP AS A LIMITED COMPANY

Legal responsibilities

There are many legal responsibilities involved with being a director and running a limited company. As a director of a limited company, the law says you must:

- Try to make the company a success, using your skills, experience and judgment
- Follow the company's rules, shown in its articles of association
- Make decisions for the benefit of the company, not yourself
- Tell other shareholders if you might personally benefit from a transaction the company makes
- Keep company records and report changes to Companies House and HM Revenue and Customs (HMRC)
- Make sure the company's accounts are a 'true and fair view' of the business' finances
- Register for Self Assessment and send a personal Self Assessment tax return every year

You can hire other people to manage some of these things day-to-day (e.g. an accountant) but you're still legally responsible for your company's records, accounts and performance.

WARNING: You may be personally liable for your company's business liabilities and be fined, prosecuted or disqualified as a company director if you don't follow the rules. Contact your professional adviser or trade association to find out more.

Limited by shares

Most limited companies are 'limited by shares'.

This means that the shareholders' responsibilities for the company's financial liabilities are limited to the value of shares that they own but haven't paid for.

Example

A company limited by shares issues 100 shares valued at £1 each when it's set up. Its 2 shareholders own 50 shares each and have both paid in full for 25 of these.

If the company goes bust, the maximum the shareholders have to pay towards its outstanding bills is £50 - the value of the remaining 25 shares that they've each not paid for.

Company directors aren't personally responsible for debts the business can't pay if it goes wrong, as long as they haven't broken the law.

Other types of company

Most companies are private companies limited by shares. There are 3 other types.

- Private company limited by guarantee - Directors or shareholders financially back the organisation up to a specific amount if things go wrong.
- Private unlimited company - Directors or shareholders are liable for all debts if things go wrong.
- Public limited company - Companies where shares are traded publicly on a market, like the London Stock Exchange.

How to set up your limited company

You must set up the company with Companies House and let HM Revenue and Customs (HMRC) know when the company starts business activities.

Every financial year, the company must:

> - Put together statutory accounts
> - Send Companies House an annual return
> - Send HMRC a Company Tax Return

The company must register for VAT if you expect its takings to be more than £81,000 a year.

If you're a director of a limited company, you must:

> - Fill in a Self Assessment tax return every year
> - Pay tax and National Insurance through the PAYE system if the company pays you a salary

Taking money out of a limited company

As a director of a limited company, you can take money from the company in 3 ways.

Salary, expenses and benefits

If you want the company to pay you a salary, expenses or benefits, you must register the company as an employer with HM Revenue and Customs (HMRC).

The company must take Income Tax and National Insurance contributions from your salary payments and pay these to HMRC, along with employers' National Insurance contributions.

Dividends

A dividend is a payment a company can make to shareholders if it has made enough profit.

You can't count dividends as business costs when you work out your Corporation Tax.

Your company mustn't pay out more in dividends than its available profits from current and previous financial years.
You must usually pay dividends to all shareholders.

To pay a dividend, you must:

- Hold a directors' meeting to 'declare' the dividend
- Keep minutes of the meeting, even if you're the only director

Dividend paperwork

For each dividend payment the company makes, you must write up a dividend voucher showing the:

- Date
- Company name
- Names of the shareholders being paid a dividend
- Amount of the dividend
- The amount of the 'dividend tax credit'

Dividend tax credits

The tax credit means your company and shareholders don't need to pay tax when the dividend is paid. But shareholders may have to pay tax on it.

To work out the dividend tax credit, divide the dividend amount by 9.

Example
You want to pay a dividend of £900. Divide £900 by 9, which gives you a dividend tax credit of £100. Pay £900 to the shareholder - but add the £100 tax credit and record a total of £1,000 on the dividend voucher.

You must give a copy of the voucher to recipients of the dividend and keep a copy for your company's records.

Directors' loans

If you take more money out of a company
than you've put in - and it isn't salary or
dividend - it's called a 'directors' loan.'
If your company makes directors' loans, you
must keep records of them.

Changing your company's registered office address

You must tell Companies House if you want to
change your company's registered office
address. If the change is approved, they will
tell HM Revenue and Customs (HMRC).
Your company's new registered office
address must be in the same part of the UK
that the company was registered
(incorporated).

For example, if your company was registered
in England and Wales, the new registered
office address must be in England or Wales.

Your registered office address won't officially
change until Companies House has confirmed
it with you.

Other changes you must report

You must tell HMRC if:

- Your business' contact details change -
  e.g. your name, business name or your
  personal or trading address
- You appoint an accountant or tax
  adviser

You must tell Companies House within 14
days if you make changes to:

- Where company records are kept
- Directors or their personal details, like
  their address
- Company secretaries (appointing a
  new one or ending an existing one's
  appointment)

You must tell Companies House within a
month if you issue more shares in your
company.

Reporting changes to Companies House

You can:

- Use the Companies House online
  service
- Fill in and send paper forms

Changes that shareholders must approve

You may need to get shareholders to vote on the decision if you want to:

- Change the company name
- Remove a director
- Change the company's articles of association

This is called 'passing a resolution'. Most resolutions will need a majority to agree (called an 'ordinary resolution'). Some might require a 75% majority (called a 'special resolution').
Companies House has more details about the types of changes and resolutions you must report to them.

Your new company name won't take effect until Companies House registers it - they'll tell you when this happens.

Shareholder voting

When you're working out whether you have a majority, count the number of shares that give the owner the right to vote, rather than the number of shareholders.

You don't necessarily need to have a meeting of shareholders to pass a resolution. If the right amount of shareholders has told you they agree, you can confirm the resolution in writing. But you must write to all shareholders letting them know about the decision.

Company and Accounting records

- Keep records about the company itself
- Keep financial and accounting records

Records about the company

You must keep details of:

- Directors, shareholders and company secretaries
- The results of any shareholder votes and resolutions
- Promises for the company to repay loans at a specific date in the future ('debentures') and who they must be paid back to
- Promises the company makes for payments if something goes wrong and it's the company's fault
- Transactions when someone buys shares in the company.

> - Loans or mortgages secured against the company's assets

You must tell Companies House if you keep the records somewhere other than the company's registered office address.

Accounting records you must keep

You must keep accounting records that include:

> - All money received and spent by the company
> - Details of assets owned by the company
> - Debts the company owes or is owed
> - Stock the company owns at the end of the financial year
> - The stock takings you used to work out the stock figure
> - All goods bought and sold
> - Who you bought and sold them to and from (unless you run a retail business)

You must also keep any other financial records; information and calculations you need to complete your Company Tax Return. If you don't keep accounting records, you can be fined £3,000 by HM Revenue and Customs

(HMRC) or disqualified as a company director.

How long to keep records

You must normally keep records for at least 6 years from the end of the last company financial year they relate to.

You may need to keep records longer if:

- They show a transaction that covers more than one of the company's accounting periods
- The company has bought something that it expects to last more than 6 years, like equipment or machinery
- You sent your Company Tax Return late
- HMRC have started a compliance check into your Company Tax Return

Company Annual Return

You must send Companies House a company annual return every year, within 28 days of the anniversary of the company's incorporation. You can send the company annual return online. It costs £13 to send online. You can also fill in and send the company annual return on paper using form

AR01. It costs £40 if you want to send paper forms.

If you miss the deadline, Companies House can close down your company or prosecute you. You could also be disqualified from being a company director.

What the company annual return must include

- The company's registered office address
- What type of business the company runs (e.g. retail, accountancy, catering)
- The address where the company's list of shareholders is kept
- The type of limited company (e.g. limited by shares, limited by guarantee)
- Name and address of all company directors (and company secretary if you have one)
- The number and value of shares issued by the company and who owns them
- Where details of 'debentures' (a type of loan the company has taken out with a promise to repay at a specific time in the future) are kept

Signs

You must display a sign showing your company name at your registered company address and wherever your business operates. If you're running your business from home, you don't need to display a sign there.

Example
If you're running three shops and an office that's not at your home, you must display a sign at each of them.
The sign must be easy to read and to see at any time, not just when you're open.

Stationery and promotional material

You must include your company's name on all company documents, publicity and letters.
On business letters, order forms, invoices and websites, you must show:

- The company's registered number
- Its registered office address
- Where the company is registered (England and Wales, Scotland or Northern Ireland)
- The fact that it's a limited company (usually by spelling out the company's full name including 'Limited' or 'Ltd')

If you want to include directors' names, you must list all of them.

If you want to show your company's share capital (how much the shares were worth when you issued them), you must say how much is 'paid up' (owned by shareholders).

SETTING UP AS A BUSINESS PARTNERSHIP

When you set up a business partnership you need to:

- Choose a name
- Choose a 'nominated partner'
- Register with HM Revenue and Customs (HMRC)

You must choose a 'nominated partner'. This is the partner who will be responsible for keeping business records and managing tax returns.
The rules are different for limited liability partnerships and limited partnerships.

Registration for the nominated partner

The nominated partner must register the partnership with HM Revenue and Customs. When they do this, they will automatically register personally for Self Assessment.

Registration for other partners

You must register for Self Assessment to pay your personal tax and National Insurance on

your share of the partnership's profit as soon as possible after you start trading.
If you register the partnership or individual partners later than 5 October in your business' second tax year, you could be charged a penalty.

Example
If you start a partnership or become a partner during tax year 2013 to 2014, you must register before 5 October 2014.

Partnerships' tax responsibilities

The nominated partner must send a partnership Self Assessment tax return every year.

All the partners must:

- Send a personal Self Assessment tax return every year
- Pay Income Tax on their share of the partnership's profits
- Pay National Insurance

The partnership will also have to register for VAT if you expect its takings to be more than £81,000 a year.

Limited liability partnerships

The partners in a limited liability partnership aren't personally liable for debts the business can't pay. Their liability is limited to the amount of money they invest in the business. Professional services firms, like solicitors or accountants, most often set up limited liability partnerships.
The Companies House website has information about how to set up a limited liability partnership.

Limited partnerships

The liability for debts that can't be paid in a limited partnership is unequally shared by its partners. This means:

- 'General' partners can be personally liable for all the partnerships' debts
- 'Limited' partners are only liable up to the amount they initially invest in the business

The Companies House website has information about how to set up a limited partnership.

Tax for limited liability and limited partnerships

Every year, the partnership must send a partnership Self Assessment tax return to HM Revenue and Customs (HMRC).
All the partners must:

> - Send a personal Self Assessment tax return every year
> - Pay Income Tax on their share of the partnership's profits
> - Pay National Insurance

Name your partnership

You can use your own names or trade under a business name. See chapter SETTING UP AS A SOLE TRADER for further advice.

Include all the partners' names and any business name on official paperwork like invoices and letters.

Partnership tax return

As the nominated partner you'll get a letter from HM Revenue and Customs (HMRC) in April or May telling you to send a partnership tax return.

You can either complete the return:

> - Online - you'll need to buy software
> - On paper - download form SA800 if HMRC hasn't sent you one

Let each partner know their share of the profits and losses so they can fill in their own tax return.

Deadlines

Send the partnership tax return by the usual Self Assessment deadlines.
If any of the partners are a company the deadline for:

> - Online returns is 31 January following the end of the tax year (or 12 months from the partnership's accounting date if later)
> - Paper returns is 31 October following the end of the tax year (or 9 months from the partnership's accounting date if later)

All the partners can be charged a penalty if the partnership tax return is late.

Record keeping

You need to keep your records for 4 years after 31 January following the end of the tax year.

Changes to the partnership

You need to tell HM Revenue and Customs (HMRC) about certain changes within a partnership.

If a partner joins or leaves

If someone joins they need to be registered for Self Assessment.

You don't need to let HMRC know if they're already registered unless the partnership is VAT registered.

If the partnership is VAT registered you must let HMRC know within 30 days every time a partner joins or leaves - you may be fined if you don't. Tell them using form VAT 2.
When a partner leaves they still need to submit a Self Assessment tax return for the year they leave.
Changes to a partnership may affect each partner's assets and the tax due on them. Record the changes in the partnership tax return and in each partner's Self Assessment return.

Changes of name or address

Log in to Self Assessment online to report a change in your partnership's name or address or contact HMRC.

If you're VAT registered you must also use VAT online services to report a change within 30 days or you may be fined. You must also report changes to the names or addresses of any of the partners.

Changing the nominated partner

Let HMRC know that the nominated partner has changed when you do the partnership tax return.

Close a partnership

The nominated partner needs to send a partnership tax return for the final period of trading as one of the tasks when closing a partnership.

EMPLOYER'S LIABILITY INSURANCE

You must get Employers' Liability (EL) insurance as soon as you become an employer - your policy must cover you for at least £5 million and come from an authorised insurer.

EL insurance will help you pay compensation if an employee is injured or becomes ill because of the work they do for you.

You may not need EL insurance if you only employ a family member or someone who is based abroad.

You can be fined £2,500 for every day you are not properly insured.

You can also be fined £1,000 if you do not display your EL certificate or refuse to make it available to inspectors when they ask.

Check to see if your insurer is authorised by looking at the Financial Conduct Authority register or contact the Financial Conduct Authority.

You may want to use an insurance broker to help you buy EL.

230

Setting up a Business in the UK

When you start a business in the UK you must choose a structure for your business.
Most businesses in the UK are:

* Sole traders
* Limited companies
* Partnerships

You must register as 'self-employed' if you are a sole trader - this means that you are working for yourself, not for someone else. Usually, if you carry on a business in the UK you'll need to live in the UK. If your business is a private limited company, you'll also need a registered office and at least 1 director in the UK.
You will then need to register your business in the UK.

Registering As An Overseas Company

If you are expanding your business to the UK and want to carry out business from an address in the UK you must register your business with Companies House.

Licences

When setting up business in the UK you may need to apply for a licence, depending on what your business is.

Setting Up A Bank Account

To set up a bank account for your business in the UK you can either:

- Open a new account in the UK
- Use the account you already have in your country
- Open a UK sterling account in your country

It may be cheaper to open a UK account or to set up a UK sterling account with your own bank, to avoid transaction and currency exchange fees.
You'll need a UK address before opening a UK bank account.

National Insurance

You may need to pay National Insurance contributions if you're self-employed, depending on how much you earn.
You may also need to deduct National Insurance contributions from any employees' wages and pay those as well.

If you're employing workers from the European Economic Area (EEA) or Switzerland, and they have an A1 form, you'll have to deduct according to the rules of their home country and not pay National Insurance contributions.

VAT

You must register for VAT with HM Revenue and Customs (HMRC) if your business turnover is more than £81,000.

Employing People

The same basic employment terms and conditions apply to all workers in the UK even if you bring those workers to the UK from another country, e.g. you must pay your workers at least the National Minimum Wage (NMW).

Employing People In The UK

You must have a contract with your employees that sets out your employees':

- Employment conditions
- Rights
- Responsibilities
- Duties

Bringing Workers To The UK

Before you bring a worker from another country you need to check they're allowed to work in the UK. You'll need to see documents to prove this.

Sponsoring Temporary Workers

You may be able to sponsor workers to come and work in the UK.
To do so you need a licence.
As a sponsor it's your responsibility to make sure your workers continue to be eligible to work in the UK and that immigration controls are followed.

Help on starting and running a business

Business Support Helpline
Telephone: 0300 456 3565
Textphone: 0208 742 8620
Monday to Friday, 9am to 6pm
Business Wales Helpline
Telephone: 0300 060 3000
Monday to Friday, 8am to 6pm
Business Gateway (Scotland)
Telephone: 0845 609 6611
Textphone: 0141 952 7053
Monday to Friday, 8am to 6pm
Invest Northern Ireland
Telephone: 0800 181 4422
Monday to Friday, 8am to 5pm

EVENT RISK ASSESSMENT

A full risk assessment should be carried out for all events. This will be a legal requirement in many circumstances. The following guidance should aid you in carrying out your risk assessments. A form to record your findings has also been provided.

Identifying the hazards

All hazards should be identified including those relating to the individual activities and equipment. A hazard is something with the potential to cause harm. Only note hazards that could result in significant harm. The following should be taken into account:

- Any slipping, tripping or falling hazards
- Hazards relating to fire risks or fire evacuation procedures
- Any chemicals or other substances hazardous to health e.g. dust or fumes
- Moving parts of machinery
- Any vehicles on site
- Electrical safety e.g. use of any portable electrical appliances
- Manual handling activities

- High Noise Levels
- Poor lighting, heating or ventilation
- Any possible risk from specific demonstrations or activities
- Crowd intensity and pinch points

This list is by no means exhaustive and care should be taken to identify any other hazards associated with the activities at the event.

Identifying those at risk

For each hazard identified, list all those who may be affected. Do not list individuals by name, just list groups of people. The following should be taken into account:

- Stewards
- Employees
- Volunteers
- Contractors
- Vendors, exhibitors and performers
- Members of the public
- Disabled persons
- Children and elderly persons
- Potential trespassers
- Expectant mothers
- Local residents

Areas to consider

- Type of event
- Potential major incidents
- Site hazards, including car parks
- Types of attendees such as children, elderly persons and the disabled
- Crowd control, capacity, access and egress and stewarding
- Provision for the emergency services
- Provision of first aid
- Provision of facilities
- Fire, security and cash collection
- Health and safety issues
- Exhibitors and demonstrations
- Amusements and attractions
- Structures
- Waste management

Assessing the risk

- The extent of the risk arising from the hazards identified must be evaluated and existing control measures taken into account. The risk is the likelihood of the harm arising from the hazard. You should list the existing controls and assess whether or not any further controls are required. The following should be taken into account:

- Any information, instruction and training regarding the event and activities involved
- Compliance with the legislative standards, codes of good practice and British Standards
- Whether or not the existing controls have reduced have reduced the risk as far as is reasonably practicable

Further action necessary to control the risk

Classify risks into high, medium and low. Examples of risks falling into these categories are as follows:

High An unsecured inflatable being used in adverse weather conditions by young children

Medium A display of animals in a roped off area

Low A mime artist performing amongst the crowd

For each risk consider whether or not it can be eliminated completely. If it cannot, then decide what must be done to reduce it to an acceptable level. Only use personal protective equipment as a last resort when there is nothing else you can reasonably do.

Consider the following:

> - Removal of the hazard
> - Preventing access to the hazard e.g. by guarding dangerous parts of machinery
> - Implement procedures to reduce exposure to the hazard
> - The use of personal protective equipment
> - Find a substitute for that activity/machine etc

Record the risk assessment findings

Use the attached Risk Assessment Form to record all significant hazards, the nature and extent of the risks and the action required to control them. Keep this for future reference or use. You could also refer to other documents you may have, such as manuals, codes of practice, etc.

Review and revise

If the nature of the risks changes during the planning of the event, the risk assessments will need to be reviewed and updated.

Information

Where the risk assessment has identified significant risks, you must provide information to all those affected, regarding the nature of the risk and the control measure to be implemented.

AFTERWORD

So now you have the benefit of what I know and how I used it to create and maintain a successful event industry company for twenty years and counting.

You may have found every word to be an invaluable tool with which to build your event industry empire, or you may have simply found a handful of golden nuggets that shine out from the rest, but what you hold in your hands is over twenty years of business experience in a very lucrative industry.

At Gala Tent, we're always looking to make great new friends and build interesting and mutually beneficial business relationships, and by picking up and reading this book, you're already one step closer to forging a new career where you're never told what to do, and you get the opportunity to run your business YOUR WAY.

Our expert sales team are available to call and have a discussion about anything that you've found in this book that piques your interest, so what are you waiting for? I look forward to hearing from you, and to becoming a part of your adventure in business success.

CONNECT WITH THE AUTHOR

www.facebook.com/jason.mace

www.facebook.com/galatents

www.twitter.com/mrjasonmace

www.linkedin.com/in/jasonmace

www.instagram.com/mrjasonmace

www.galatent.co.uk

Printed in Great Britain
by Amazon